CONSCIOUSNESS
EXPLAINED BETTER

towards an integral understanding of the
multifaceted nature of consciousness

OMEGA BOOKS

The OMEGA BOOKS series from Paragon House is dedicated to classic and contemporary works about human development and the nature of ultimate reality, encompassing the fields of mysticism and spirituality, enlightenment, the evolution of consciousness, and the human potential for self-directed growth in body, mind, and spirit.

John White, M.A.T., Series Editor of OMEGA BOOKS, is an internationally known author, editor, and educator in the fields of consciousness research and higher human development.

MORE TITLES IN OMEGA BOOKS

CONSCIOUSNESS
EXPLAINED BETTER

towards an integral understanding of the
multifaceted nature of consciousness

by
ALLAN COMBS

PARAGON HOUSE
St. Paul, Minnesota

First Edition 2009

Published in the United States by
Paragon House
1925 Oakcrest Avenue
St. Paul, MN 55113

Library of Congress Cataloging-in-Publication Data

Combs, Allan, 1942-
  Consciousness explained better : towards an integral understanding of the multifaceted nature of consciousness / by Allan Combs. -- 1st ed.
    p. cm.
  Includes bibliographical references.
  Summary: "Consciousness is explored as a living stream of lucid experience composed of the essence of the moments of our lives. Grounded in Ken Wilber's model, consciousness is explained from many points of view: its historical evolution, its growth in the individual, its mystical dimensions, and the meaning of enlightenment"--Provided by publisher.
  ISBN 978-1-55778-883-2 (pbk. : alk. paper)
  1. Consciousness. I. Title.
  B808.9.C63 2009
  126--dc22
                          2009018922

Renderings of art courtesy of Monica Combs. Used with permission.
Cover image courtesy of Mardi Ahmed © 2005. See www.mardi.ca.
Photographed by Keith Shaw. See www.keithshawphotography.com.

The paper used in this publication meets the minimum requirements of American National Standard for Information Sciences—Permanence of Paper for Printed Library Materials, ANSIZ39.48-1984.

Manufactured in the United States of America
10 9 8 7 6 5 4 3 2 1

For current information about all releases from Paragon House,
visit the web site at http://www.paragonhouse.com

APPRECIATIONS

To Ed Mulligan for starting me down the path of authorship. To Jeffery Martin, Bill Crandall, Jonathan Bricklin, and Larry Van Pelt for editorial help and suggestions. And to my wife, Julie, for her kind patience and caring support.

To my loving daughters:
Monica Combs, artist, for creating the minimalist art renderings herein.
Mollie Dezern, art historian, for advice on copyrights.

And to Ken Wilber for suggesting this book in the first place, and for sharing his friendship and advice throughout its writing.

The universe evolves in consciousness of itself and causes itself to be. We are just this blessed consciousness, nothing more and nothing less. We are the light inside light that fuses into the atoms of our bodies; we are the fire that whirls across the stellar deeps and dances all things into being.

—*David Zindell*[1]

CONTENTS

Tables

Figures

FOREWORD

The "problem" of consciousness—and its attendant "problem," the nature of reality, or what we are conscious *of* and perhaps what *makes* us conscious—marks the frontier of human exploration, a frontier that we may never fully conquer. Empiricism, the method most used in recent years in the West, may be inadequate to penetrate the mystery. Centuries of idealist philosophy and contemplative practice have produced interesting results but are limited by their own particular paradigms. Indeed, it is hard even to know how to define the problem, and therefore to determine what would constitute a satisfactory "solution."

Attempts to understand consciousness from the scientific paradigm are concerned with predictability and the ability to design, especially to improve. Solutions from this perspective would explain causal relations and provide an ability to control and shape them. Attempts to understand from the philosophical and contemplative paradigm are concerned with ultimate meaning and right living. Solutions from this perspective are more about understanding and alignment.

Either way, the urge to understand involves improving the quality of life for the greater good. But what makes solving the problem of consciousness so compelling is essentially personal: it would bring meaning for each one of us. It would answer those gnawing existential questions about who we are, how the world works, and what is "real." It would therefore tell us how to live and make sense of our lives. We are compelled to wonder about these things *because* we are conscious—and from a developmental perspective—*to the degree* that we are conscious.

This subjectivity and centrality to the meaning of life is why we persevere in the quest for consciousness. The wonderful part of consciousness is both its (presumed) universality and its precious subjectivity. Consciousness is fundamentally about what's out *there* as well as what's in *here*, and what's in here is, so far as we know, uniquely ours: the private, idiosyncratic, historical world of our own endlessly fascinating subjectivity. As we unfold to ourselves and the world unfolds to us, we experience ourselves as conscious. But to what extent is any of this real, illusory, or even the experience of any other entity we perceive? Are we alone in our own solipsistic world, or is the experience of consciousness something we share with those we are pleased to consider sentient beings? Or with everything, including inanimate objects and the smallest particles of matter? Or is it the very fabric of the cosmos, the Absolute?

Time, space, perspective, matter, agency: all of these enormities are part of the problem of consciousness. Little wonder humanity has made so little progress in finding the solutions, although it has perhaps done a little better in recognizing some of the parts of the problem.

Consciousness Explained Better is a unique contribution. This compact volume represents thousands of years of humanity's struggle to understand consciousness from a wide variety of perspectives. It is an up-to-date digest of the search in bite-sized chapters. Allan Combs has managed to encapsulate and synthesize vast bodies of thought and research without dilution. He has made even the most mind-twisting arguments and questions comprehensible, and he has brought forward scholarship and rigorous inquiry in language that speaks to the heart as well as the head. This book satisfies with its comprehensiveness yet intrigues with all that still remains enigmatic. It brings forward the yearning, the brilliance, the awe, and the outrageous audacity of our search to understand consciousness. It reminds us that, in a world where much of our lives is reduced to the trivial, the logistical, and the manageable, everything about that world and about ourselves is still completely beyond our grasp. We still live and move in the Great Mystery.

Jenny Wade
Author, *Changes of Mind* and *Transcendent Sex*

INTRODUCTION

This book is about consciousness.

I've been interested in consciousness for nearly my whole life, because to me it is the essence of what I am, and of what you are, and of what it is to be human and what it is to be alive. Aware, awake, what it is like to be me, right now, and right here. Present. For me it is the very heart, soul, and substance of all that is spiritual, the key to the greatest mystery of all, and the plainest and simplest fact in the world.

Let me put it this way. Consciousness is the background, or simply the ground, of all experience. Whatever experience you have, whether it is a high mystical rapture, an abysmal depression, an explosive sexual ecstasy, the sight of a bright twinkling star in a dark night sky, the sound of thunder, the taste of honey, or the scent of sandalwood, it all unfolds in an already dimensionless field of perfect emptiness that is the open shining ground that lurks behind and permeates all of experience. It is consciousness.

The study of consciousness had a rough time of it during most of the twentieth century, at least in philosophy and psychology. This was not the case a hundred years ago. The great explorers of the consciousness at the *fin de siècle* such as Franz Brentano in Germany, William James and James Mark Baldwin in the United States, and F.W.H. Myers in England, all viewed consciousness as a dynamic stream of experience with both conscious and unconscious aspects, and which very likely continued on in one form or another after death. They studied and honored the widest ranges of human experience, extending from pathology to profound mysticism. Their students and younger colleagues included such names as Sigmund Freud, Carl Jung, Edmund Husserl, and Jean Piaget.

Unfortunately, the incredibly creative stream of scholarship that flowed from these pioneers came to a virtual stop after the First World War. There were many reasons for this, including the growing influence of Logical Positivism with its emphasis on explicit and public observation as a feature of valid science, and along with this the *Unity of Science* movement, stressing the objective observation of material events as a global scientific agenda. And it seemed the war itself had produced an austere attitude through all fields of scholarship that stressed no-nonsense practical approaches to inquiry and discouraged the investigation of seemingly ephemeral topics such as consciousness. In psychology as well as philosophy, behaviorism became a dominant theme which, in its most extreme form, even denied the existence of consciousness.

By the 1960s the most reductive versions of this kind of thinking were finally waning, but were soon replaced by another kind of reductionist paradigm, that of the *cognitive sciences*. These permeated virtually every field of inquiry from psychology and philosophy to linguistics and biology. The basic premise was that everything works on information. Now, information as something quantifiable, something you could write equations about and mold in sophisticated ways, was first invented by communications researchers during World War II. It soon became the basis for understanding and designing computers, which were increasingly thought of as self-governing or *cybernetic* machines. Before long it became apparent to reductionist thinking philosophers and scientists alike that the human brain is such a cybernetic machine—a three pound on-board computer—and that the best way to understand it, and the mind as well, was to view them as information processing devices, or in other words computers. Thus, the cognitive approach to understanding the mind and the brain is to view them as if they were computers running programs, or in artificial intelligence terms, *algorithms*.

At about the same time there began a slow re-discovery of consciousness. Starting in the 1960s, and increasingly through the 1980s and 1990s and on into the new millennium consciousness slowly regained its status as a legitimate topic in academic and research settings. The problem, however, was that along the way it had been reconceptualized into cognitive terms, that is, into information and computer language. The "computational brain" became a key phrase for the 1980s, and the "neural network brain" for the 1990s and even today. In the meantime "analytical philosophy," the dominant philosophical style of the English-speaking world, and a style that placed great emphasis on logical and reductionistic analyses, found easy purchase on the cognitive science approach. Soon the majority of philosophers, psychologists, and brain scientists interested in consciousness and the mind came to rely on this analytical style of thinking.

Unfortunately, analytic philosophy, at least in the view of this writer, is more appropriate for solving chess problems than for understanding of the nuances of consciousness. The problem is not so much whether the brain actually works like a computer as whether this is a useful way to understand consciousness. Daniel Dennett is perhaps the best known and most widely read exponent of the analytical approach. His 1992 classic, *Consciousness Explained*, is over five hundred pages of tortuous symbolic reasoning. Many readers, including some other philosophers, have thrown the book down, renaming it "Consciousness Explained Away." The late Nobel laureate Francis Crick, himself a thorough-going reductionist, observed of it, "Dennett is over-persuaded by his own elegance."

All this is to say that while late twentieth-century philosophy, psychology, and even neurology have again taken a serious hold of the topic of consciousness, they have treated it harshly at best, pushing it onto the Procrustean beds of their own currently fashionable paradigms. The great researchers a hundred years ago had pursued the topic of consciousness in quite a different spirit, embracing it in a combination of open-minded sophistication and wide-eyed curiosity that we have hardly seen since.[2]

The approach to consciousness I have taken in this book is to reach back again to the style of the great *fin de siècle* explorers such as William James and Mark Baldwin in an attempt to recapture afresh the mystery, excitement, and wealth of its study and to do so, however, without overlooking the many useful discoveries made since that time.

I hope that for some this book will also serve as an introduction to Ken Wilber's thinking on many aspects of the topic of consciousness. He and I have shared a passion for understanding the essence of consciousness for many years. Though we have worked independently for much of that time we share many ideas in common. For me it has been a great help to position my own thinking in the much larger and more comprehensive conceptual framework that Wilber has created. It has provided a generous and, in my view, enormously creative context for framing my own thought.

Welcome.

1. A Word Worn Smooth by a Million Tongues[1]

What a world of unseen visions and heard silences, this insubstantial country of the mind! What ineffable essences, these touchless rememberings and unshowable reveries! And the privacy of it all! A secret theater of speechless monologue and prevenient counsel, an invisible mansion of all moods, musings, and mysteries, an infinite resort of disappointments and discoveries. A whole kingdom where each of us reigns reclusively alone, questioning what we will, commanding what we can. A hidden hermitage where we may study out the troubled book of what we have done and yet may do. An introcosm that is more myself than anything I can find in a mirror. This consciousness that is myself of selves, that is everything, and yet nothing at all—what is it?

—*Julian Jaynes* [2]

I hate to break this news so soon, but the truth is there is no such thing as consciousness, at least not in the sense we usually think of it. It is better we get off on the right foot, so let me explain.

The word *consciousness* is of fairly recent origin, dating back only a few hundred years. Its Latin predecessor was the word *conscientia*, which all the way back in Roman jurisprudence referred to the knowledge a witness has of the deeds of another person. The implication was that this knowledge was supposed to be "shared with" others, for example, in court. Later the word was used by medieval Christian scholars to mean something very much like a *moral conscience*. In the thirteenth century Thomas Aquinas used it to indicate the application of practical moral knowledge to the making of personal decisions. It was not until the middle of the seventeenth century that René Descartes used *conscientia* in a modern way to refer to an awareness of inner ideas, thoughts, and images.[3] He attributed these to an inner reality or mind-stuff, *res cogitans*, which he sharply distinguished from the world of "extended" material objects, *res extensa*. Influenced by Descartes' writings the British philosopher John Locke soon went the whole way with the notion of inner experiences, arguing that everything we know comes to us as *sensations* which, when we reflect upon them, give birth to simple and complex ideas in the mind.[4] According to Locke every bit of knowledge we acquire during our lifetime comes to us, in one way or another, through the senses.[5] The important point here is the extent to which Locke emphasized inner experiences of the mind as the only reliable basis for knowledge. "It is evident the mind knows not things immediately, but only by intervention of the ideas it has of them."[6] In other words, only sensory impressions molded into mental ideas give birth to knowledge, so in reality we know nothing directly about the world in which we live. This idea is at the root of British Empiricism, and it is not too surprising that other empiricists such as the Irish Bishop George Berkeley soon put forward surprisingly convincing arguments to the effect that there is no outside world at all!

Now, let's take a closer look. What we see is that Descartes' notion of mind-stuff combines with Locke's focus on the mind as the only source of direct experience to create a powerful sense of an inner consciousness that is *something real in its own right*. It has properties and a life of its own that could, and has to this very day, been appraised, assessed, celebrated, and surveyed by a legion of philosophers and scientists of all kinds.[7]

But what is wrong with this picture? One could fill libraries with the works of philosophers who have criticized Descartes' dualism of mind and body. Some have argued that only the material world exists (which includes the human brain and body) and that consciousness and the mind are simply illusions, ephemeral productions of the neurochemistry of the brain. Others have argued in favor of views that allow for the reality of consciousness, but assign it any of a number of influential or uninfluential positions with regard to the body and brain. Let's cut through all that, however, and get straight to the point. No one but a lunatic would argue that when we look into our own thoughts, feelings, and remembrances, we find nothing there. Indeed, we experience the richness of our own inner dimensions every moment of our lives. We are rich with experiences of our inner lives as well as the outer world.

The problem comes when we add in a new element and call it "consciousness." There is no question that we *experience* things all the time. For instance, I might experience an itch on the top of my right foot. I say that I feel the itch, that the itch has captured my attention. I am itching, or even that I am conscious of the itching. Note, however, that the latter use of the word "conscious" is as an adverb that portrays the verb "itching." Now here comes the rub. When I say this itch has "entered my consciousness," as if consciousness was something real beyond the itch itself; or if I say that "I have consciousness" (and can therefore feel the itch), I am adding extra complication to the simple experience of itching. I am claiming the existence of something called *consciousness*, which at this point has become a noun.

Stick with me now; I am not alone in this view. After spending the first half of his career exploring the nature of consciousness, the pioneer American psychologist and philosopher William James had this to say:

> For twenty years past I have mistrusted 'consciousness' as an entity; for seven or eight years past I have suggested its non-existence to my students, and tried to give them its pragmatic equivalent in realities of experience. It seems time that the hour is ripe for it to be openly and universally discarded.[8]

See? Let's follow James a bit further:

> To deny …that 'consciousness' exists seems…absurd on the face of it … Let me then immediately explain that I mean only to deny that the word stands for an entity... There is, I mean, no aboriginal stuff or quality of being, contrasted with that of which material objects are made, out of which our thoughts of them are made.[9]

We humans seem to have a basic need to understand the world in terms of objects and things. For example, we give names to processes and events and soon begin to think of them as *things*. Water flowing over a cliff becomes a *waterfall*. Wind and rain become a *storm*. Talking this way is useful and has many advantages, but can confuse us into thinking that what we have now named is a real thingamajig, somehow more than its components of, say, water flowing, or wind and rain.[10] I am reminded of the story about a father who took his son to their first baseball game. Though the boy enjoyed the game greatly, afterward he appeared confused. When his father asked what was wrong he said, "Father, I saw players. I saw the uniforms. I saw the bats and I saw the dugouts. I also heard about the team spirit, but I never saw it. Where was the team spirit?" Of course the team spirit is not some creature that can be seen prowling the streets long after that game is over, any more than a waterfall can be carried away from the river! In both instances the naming of nouns—*team spirit* and *waterfall*—is simply a convenient way of speaking. If we think that they indicate real *things* we would be mistaken. *Consciousness* is the same way.

Philosopher Alfred North Whitehead called the mistake of making a process into a thing "misplaced concreteness." Because this notion is so important for our understanding of consciousness please bear with me through one more example. Long before Newton's day it was well known by everyone that when objects are shoved off tables or dropped out of trees they fall down. Newton did not discover this fact. Rather, he did discover that falling follows a regular pattern, which later came to be known as the "law of gravity." The term "law" seemed appropriate at the time because it was widely believed that God had made the universe just as it is, imbuing it with the rules (laws) that He himself had crafted.[11] The point here is that people soon started thinking of gravity, not as a regularity in the way things fall down, but rather as a palpable "force" in its own right. Newton himself made this mistake and worried over it a great deal.[12] Gravity had become a *thing*. There are many such examples in science. Sometimes they are very useful, as is the case with gravity. But as you can see from just about any survey of formal or popular writings on the topic of gravity, physicists are still in a muddle to figure out exactly what it is.

Consciousness is in the same boat. Descartes and Locke's association of this word with our inner worlds of thought, sensation, and perception, created the illusion that consciousness was only on the *inside* and not the *outside*. As we have seen, this put the source of all knowledge on the inside as well. It followed from this that knowledge of the outer world is possible only as an inner reflection seen through the mirror of the senses.[13]

Such a view gives one the feeling of a warm personal interior against a cold objective and material world outside. I am reminded of a poem about mittens:

> He killed the noble Mudjokivis.
> Of the skin he made him mittens,
> Made them with the fur side inside,
> Made them with the skin side outside.
> He, to get the warm side inside,
> Put the inside skin side outside;
> He, to get the cold side outside,
> Put the warm side fur side inside.
> That's why he put the fur side inside,
> Why he put the skin side outside,
> Why he turned them inside outside.
>
> —*Anonymous* [14]

For those of us who are introverts the inside indeed seems warm and fuzzy compared to the outside. But both qualify as experience, and only the contortions of an overly busy philosophical mind can elevate one above the other. Indeed, James argued in his philosophy of *radical empiricism* that both are essentially equivalent. We merely assign some experiences to our "inner life" and some to the "outside world." Unfortunately, he died before he could make a complete case for an even-handed view of the world as pure experience. In this book, however, I hope to avoid philosophical contortions and stick to common sense as much as possible. Common sense tells us that we have experiences of objects and events that populate an objective outside world, and likewise we have experiences of thoughts, feelings, and reflections that populate our inner world. These are the facts given to us by day to day experience, and unless we are absorbed in philosophically abstruse thought or caught up in mystical rapture they can hardly be denied.

James eventually abandoned the word *consciousness* completely, substituting the word *experience*. Everything else remained the same. As you know, I agree with this decision whenever the word *consciousness* is used as a noun, that is, when its use implies the existence of some substance or other reality beyond the bare fact of experiencing inner or outer events. But let me hasten to say that I have no objection to its use in other ways, such as "ecological consciousness," "multicultural consciousness," or being "conscious of" something, say, the kindness of a friend. The latter instance refers to being *aware* of the friend's kindness. This is also the way psychologists often use "consciousness" to talk about a person's awareness of themselves. For example, it might be said that, "John is not conscious of the fact he is self-centered and obnoxious!" Physicians say people are "conscious" (awake) as opposed to "unconscious" (asleep, in a coma, etc.) if after a car accident they can tell you their name and address. All these uses are fine with me. I only draw the line when someone starts talking about the "nature of consciousness," its "properties," and so on, all suggesting it is a thing in itself.

But all the above in the balance, it seems clear that something is amiss with our ordinary notion of consciousness and, without putting too fine a point on it, with the usual philosophical ideas about it as well. Since this is a book about consciousness I hope to set this situation right—not by posing yet another argument about the essential nature of consciousness, its relationship or lack of relationship to the body and the brain, or by claiming it does not exist or, contrariwise, that nothing else exists, but by offering a radically new way understanding it. Bear with me for another chapter or so while we come to understand the object of our investigation a bit better before we jump in head over heels to a new way of thinking about it.

2. Never at Rest

As we take, in fact, a general view of the wonderful stream of our consciousness, what strikes us first is this different pace of its parts. Like a bird's life, it seems to be made of an alternation of flights and perchings. The rhythm of language expresses this, where every thought is expressed in a sentence, and every sentence closed by a period. The resting-places are usually occupied by sensorial imaginations of some sort, whose peculiarity is that they can be held before the mind for an indefinite time, and contemplated without changing; the places of flight are filled with thoughts of relations, static or dynamic, that for the most part obtain between the matters contemplated in the periods of comparative rest.

—*William James* [1]

Conscious experience is like a dance in which we glide and then pause, glide and then pause. If we stop to reflect on our own awareness we capture only the moment of the pause. For example, I am now looking into the fireplace on the opposite side of my study. But I easily forget the previous glide of my attention to the fireplace from the picture of the birch log on the matchbook resting on my desk. It is a bit like trying to glance at the mirror quickly enough to catch your own image still looking somewhere else. But James has shown that we can indeed see these movements in our own shifting awareness if we submerge ourselves sufficiently in the flow.

James pointed out again and again that consciousness, which he later referred to as experience, is *continuous*. Even when dramatically new experiences seem virtually to explode into awareness, they are fused with preceding and subsequent experiences by relationships that meld them both into a single fabric. James used the example of thunder breaking into silence to make this point.

> Into the awareness of the thunder itself the awareness of
> the previous silence creeps and continues; for what we hear
> when the thunder crashes is not thunder *pure*, but thunder-
> breaking-upon-silence-and-contrasting-with-it.[2]

Again, of consciousness,

> Such words as 'chain' or 'train' do not describe it fitly... It
> is nothing jointed; it flows. A 'river' or a 'stream' are the
> metaphors by which it is most naturally described.[3]

Thus, James used two metaphors to characterize conscious experience. The first was of a flowing stream while the second was of the flights and perchings of a bird. In the latter metaphor the flights represent moments of transition between one thought and another, from one idea, recollection, sensation, or feeling, to another. The perchings occur when our awareness stops to rest in the presence of these ideas, recollections, sensations, or feelings.

James went to great pains to explain that these moments of substance are not the sum and all of experience, but are woven together in time by the relationships they hold to each other. A photograph of my grandmother, noticed on a nearby bookshelf, carries my mind away to childhood summers with her in Michigan where I swam in the icy waters of Lake Michigan, built sand palaces on sunny beaches, and spent rocking-chair evenings watching logs burn in the cabin fireplace while she read aloud. My thoughts flow from one aspect of my childhood to another until my reverie is interrupted by the reality of the computer screen before me and I realize that I came to my desk to write and not to reminisce. This dawning awareness momentarily crosses my reflections of childhood and for a moment they pass like two travelers on the same road.

My awareness of images and feelings from childhood, the sight of the computer screen before me, and taste of hot tea in the morning as I write, are all moments of substance—the perchings of conscious experience. What connects them are relationships—their similarities, contrasts, nearness in times remembered, emotional tone, and so forth—all easily overlooked but without which the stream of experience would appear a disjointed aggregate of flotsam and jetsam. Such relationships are the guide-wires on which experience glides from subject to subject. In his bird metaphor, above, James referred to such movements as "flights," or more often as *transient* moments of experience, contrasted with the stationary and sometimes lingering moments of *content*. Like a bird in flight, the transient moments are difficult to catch. To study them one must enter the stream of experience itself and observe them as James did, from the inside. If we stand back and scrutinize our experience from the outside we tend to see only the islets of content. This is exactly what René Descartes did in his highly influential *Meditations on First Philosophy*. His approach continued with philosophers such as George Berkeley and David Hume, and can be seen today in the work of philosophers of mind such as Daniel Dennett.[4]

James eventually came to refer to these islets as "buds," "drops," or "pulses" of experience, each a complete experiential event in itself. The term "bud" is especially suggestive because it implies a living process that gives birth to further experiences. Each is the product of preceding buds such as previous thoughts, memories, and sensory impressions; and it in turn contributes to the creation of future buds. Recognizing the importance of this idea, the twentieth century American philosopher Alfred North Whitehead adopted the notion of buds or drops of experience from James, placing it in a larger metaphysical vision of the entire kosmos as experience. In his principal work, *Process and Reality*, he quotes James: "[Our] acquaintance with reality grows literally by buds or drops of perception. Intellectually and on reflection you can divide these into components, but as immediately given, they come totally or not at all."[5] The point here is that a bud or drop of experience cannot be teased apart into the threads of which it is composed except by subsequent reflection. Each bud or pulse is a whole event, complete in itself. This basic idea is not limited to perception, but applies as well to all forms of experience.

In a similar spirit Whitehead introduced the term *concrescence* (from Latin meaning to "grow together") to indicate the notion that each event, each drop of experience, represents the gathering together of many preceding influences. He was speaking from his organic view of reality. For James, who was interested in the nature of personal experience, each drop, each pulsation, gathers together preceding experiences still active as residual perceptions, feelings, or thoughts at the time of the pulsation. James speculated that such residual influences remained temporarily active in the neuronal pathways of the brain to converge and erupt into awareness as buds or pulsations of experience.

Reflecting on the above ideas as well as those from the previous chapter, we see that James and Whitehead had much in common. Though James emphasized personal experience and Whitehead cosmology, both emphasized process: James with his stream of consciousness, and Whitehead with his metaphysical vision of reality itself, including the whole manifest universe. The idea that experience, individual as well as cosmic, presents itself as buds, drops, or pulsations is important in both. It is an idea indebted to the image of the bird that flits from limb to limb, and is central for both James and Whitehead. Interestingly, a similar idea is found in Buddhist phenomenology, which parses time into momentary occasions or dharmas.

Now we are ready to move on to the new ideas about consciousness promised in the last chapter.

3. The Four Streams of Experience

A universe comes into being when a space is severed.

—*G. Spencer-Brown* [1]

Four-part harmony—harmony in which each chord has four notes that create four melodic lines.

—*The Free Dictionary* [2]

In the years 1665 and 1666 the Great Plague[3] swept through the cities and towns of England. Because of it Isaac Newton abandoned his residence at Cambridge and moved to his family home at Woolsthorpe Manor in Lincolnshire. There he pursued a long-standing interest in the nature of light and color by conducting some experiments that later became landmarks in the development of both the physics of light and the scientific method as it is known today. These experiments were remarkably simple while at the same time allowing him to isolate certain features of light, and especially of color, that had never before been seen with such clarity.

Newton sealed off a room in his house so no light could enter. Then he made a small slit in a window shutter so only a single shaft of sunlight entered the room. He passed the shaft of light through a glass prism from which it emerged as a complete spectrum of colors. These could be projected onto a white screen for ease of viewing. Placing an opaque lattice such as a comb across the emerging stream of colored light broke it into smaller beams which, if the size of the lattice was properly adjusted, could be recognized as discrete colors such as red, orange, yellow, green, and blue.

Now, it turns out that when conscious experience is passed through the appropriate prism it too can be seen in multiple colors, or speaking literally, in multiple *perspectives*. This is the prism of reflective awareness by which we each can examine the facets of our own experience. In this way we will first see how consciousness bifurcates naturally into two streams of experience, then how it further divides into four streams. Later in the book we will find that passing through the proper prism of reflection it can be seen to divide again into eight streams.

Figure 3.1. Newton's Experiment

In developing an understanding of these streams I rely heavily on the work of contemporary philosopher Ken Wilber whose thinking on many of the topics in this book parallels my own. Quite a few readers will know that he and I have been friends for many years, and though we have had differences in opinion we have labored to work these out to create the clearest overall understandings.[4]

Wilber's philosophy begins with the idea that our experience is based on perceptions. To completely understand this concept we must get comfortable with the notion that conscious experience always involves some form of perception. I will not belabor this point throughout the book, but it is important to realize that our experience of ourselves and the world in which we live is a product of the ways in which we perceive them. The alternative view is what philosophers term "naïve realism," meaning the belief that reality is exactly what it appears to be. Few educated people today would accept this idea, which in European philosophy is known by the fancy name of "the myth of the given."[5] This does not mean that there is nothing to reality but experience. It just means that the immediate evidence of our senses should not be taken as the final authority on exactly how things are. This was the point of Plato's *Parable of the Cave*, in which people were chained together facing the wall of a cave so that they could see only shadows of the people passing by behind them who were carrying various objects. We need not trace the history of this problem here except to recognize that to understand the nature of conscious experience means to understand that at each moment it is grounded in our perceptions of ourselves, others, and the world around us. This will be made clear soon, so let us start at the beginning.

The first fractionation of experience by the prism of refraction divides it into an outer and an inner dimension—an outside and an inside. This may seem like a no-brainer, but recalling the lessons of the first two chapters it is apparent that even great minds have stumbled upon this issue. As we saw in chapter 1, at the very outset of modern thought, in 1640, René Descartes had begun his *Meditations on First Philosophy*[6] by questioning the truth of any experience of the objective world. Not long after that, Bishop George Berkeley had attempted to dismiss the entire material world in favor of a pure idealism supported only by the mind of God.[7] Later, John Locke had struggled to justify a science founded strictly on the observation of the objective world as it presents itself to the mind through the senses. He and other British Empiricists were so successful in this project that by the late nineteenth century the shoe was on the other foot and respectable scientists were having nothing to do with interior consciousness. Freud, Jung, and others exploring the inner worlds of mind were simply dismissed as pseudo-scientists. Even today many scientists and philosophers consider consciousness to be no more than a "ghost in the machine" of our material brains.

The second fractionation of experience by the prism of refraction divides it into singular and plural parts, or the perception of individual objects and processes on the one hand, and groups of objects and processes on the other. This too may seem about as basic as you can get, but it is more profound than it appears on first nod. A few decades back the British mathematician G. Spencer-Brown created a new and widely discussed calculus that begins with the notion of cleaving an unbroken primordial space into two separate regions, establishing an *inside* and *outside* and thereby creating a world.[8] Interestingly, the idea that the Kosmos[9] began when the primal void split to create the first distinction, thus breaking symmetry, is quite ancient and found in one form or another in almost every mystical tradition. Similarly, modern cosmology holds that the breaking of symmetry in the vast energy field that existed shortly after the Big Bang was a necessary precondition for the evolution of our universe.[10]

It is worth noting, however, that Wilber did not arrive at these distinctions—inner vs. outer and singular vs. plural—by pure philosophical speculation. The procedure he used was very concrete. Seeking a way to make sense out of the many kinds of knowledge that humankind has created, he began to sort the hundreds of articles and books he owned into stacks on the large living room floor of his Colorado home. Seeking the simplest and most basic organization possible, he sorted and re-sorted, searching for an architecture of knowledge that would accommodate virtually every realm of human inquiry. When he finished there were four stacks divided along two axes: *inner* and *outer*, and *singular* and *plural*. Thus was created the basic four-quadrant diagram published in his groundbreaking 1995 book, *Sex, Ecology, Spirituality*.

This four-quadrant approach will already be familiar to many readers. The two left-hand quadrants represent our perceptions of inner experience while the two right-hand quadrants represent our perceptions of the outer world. At the same time the two upper quadrants represent our perceptions of single objects and

I	**IT**
Interior-Individual	**Exterior-Individual**
Intentional	Behavioral
Subjective	Objective
Upper Left	**Upper Right**
WE	**ITS**
Interior-Collective	**Exterior-Collective**
Cultural	Social
Intersubjective	Interobjective
Lower Left	**Lower Right**

Figure 3.2. The Basic Four Quadrants [11]

events while the two lower quadrants represent multiple objects or events. Each quadrant represents both a broad category of knowledge and a basic dimension of the world as we perceive it. We find "I" in the upper left (UL) quadrant representing personal internal realities, and "WE" in the lower left (LL) quadrant representing shared internal realities. In the upper right (UR) quadrant we find "IT" representing single instances of objective objects and events, and in lower right (LR) "ITS" representing groups or collections of objects and events.

Expanding these ideas, the UL also represents inner subjective experiences and knowledge about such experiences. It represents our sense of self as well as knowledge about psychological structures and dynamics such as those explored by William James, Sigmund Freud, Jean Piaget, and many others. It embraces those aspects of both psychology and philosophy that focus on the inner life and its growth and development. It also includes the study of structures and states of consciousness, of which we will have much more to say in the coming pages. The LL quadrant, in contrast, represents shared knowledge and experience, including "intersubjective" experiences as well as cultural values and norms. Here we find much of traditional European structuralism, the sociology of cultural beliefs, and the problem of human communication.

Moving on to the right-hand quadrants we find the material realities of the world. Wilber has been criticized for not paying more attention to these, but he rightly points out that the bulk of traditional science already deals with them. Nevertheless, he has written a fair amount about these two quadrants and in the coming pages we will be examining them as well, especially in their relationship to conscious experience. The UR quadrant represents individual objects and events, while the LR represents whole collections of objects and events as well as their relationships to each other. Here it is useful to recall again that the quadrants are in fact perspectives. The human brain, for example, can be seen as a single organ (UR) or as a dynamically interacting set of nerve cells and neurochemicals (LR). Both are legitimate and useful yet they represent two different perspectives. To take a different example, when the equations of classical Newtonian physics are applied within the gravitational field of the Earth they easily describe the behavior of single physical bodies (UR). In space, however, they can be applied to the system of gravitational influences that two separate bodies exert on each other (LR). Interestingly, the utility of these equations is exhausted when three or more bodies are involved. More complex mathematics are then needed, involving a more sophisticated development of the LR perspective.[12]

Because the LR concerns the behavior of groups, this quadrant is often associated with systems theory or the study of the behavior of systems when viewed as a whole. There are many kinds of systems including physical ones such as the solar system, as well as electrical, biological, ecological, economic, political systems, and so on.

Quadrants vs. quadrivia

To clarify all this let's take a quick look at a concrete example. I have a small black Pug dog named Jack. I have certain thoughts and feelings about Jack (UL), most but not all of which are positive. My wife and I share the perception that Jack is an affectionate and amusing dog (LL). At the same time I cannot ignore my perception of Jack as a small but muscular physical creature (UR), and that he populates my home along with my old Labrador Retriever, making a curious little community (LR) to which, when I am feeling generous, I add myself and my wife.

Now, I assume that Jack has a similar set of perceptions, at least in his own dog-like way. He seems to have his own dog feelings and thoughts about the rest of us, and relates to us as physical creatures. It is hard to say whether he sees us as individuals or part of a community, but this does not seem to be a problem for him.

But one important point here, and an obvious one, is that inanimate objects such as stones, cell phones, computers, and book jackets, do not have such perceptions because they are not alive and are not conscious. You can look at a physical object, say your computer, from any of the four perspectives, but the computer itself does not look back at you, at least in any conscious way. Nevertheless, we have fairly complex feelings about our personal computers (UL), we seem to be in some sort of human-machine relationship with them (LL), we recognize them as a physical objects (UR), and we many have several computers in our home that are networked together for purposes of file sharing and so on (LR).

Thus, your computer can be the object of perceptions that arise from all four quadrants. But these are your quadrants and not those of the computer. It does not have quadrants because it is not a conscious being. If, however, we shift our point of view from the person perceiving to the object perceived, in this instance the computer, then we use the term *quadrivia*. The computer is seen to be the object of certain feelings by its owner (UL), is seen to be in a relationship with its owner (LL), say, for work or for entertainment, is seen as a physical object (UR), and perhaps is seen as part of a network of similar physical objects (LR). In these instances we are speaking of the quadrivia of the computer, rather than the quadrants that refer to actual streams of experience. I mention all this because discussions of Wilber's philosophy often include both quadrants and their counterparts, the quadrivia, and it is easy to find the distinction between them confusing.

Now let us move on to less abstract topics beginning with an examination of consciousness in the mind of the child.

"Will you walk a little faster?" said a whiting to a snail,

"There's a porpoise close behind us, and he's treading on my tail.

See how eagerly the lobsters and the turtles all advance!

They are waiting on the shingle—will you come and join the dance?"

—*The Lobster Quadrille* [13]

4. From One Great Blooming, Buzzing Confusion

The mind proceeds, in the pre-logical period, by the motives of memory, imagery, play, and action, achieving in its own way the use of general and abstract contents which become "notions" and "concepts," the essential instruments of reasoning...

—*James Mark Baldwin, 1930* [1]

To understand consciousness as lived experience we need look beyond abstract reflections to actual moment to moment reality. In other words, we must seek the texture of our lived experience. This texture is colored by many elements such as the flow of thoughts, memories, and feelings through our awareness as well as the kaleidoscopic flux of sounds, images, and sensations that impress themselves upon us from the external world. How all this jells together to paint for each of us a canvas of personal reality depends on a number of things, none more important than our own level of growth and maturation.

In Plato's *Phaedrus*, Socrates tells us that prior to birth the soul inhabits an ethereal realm where it possesses wings and is privy to true beauty and knowledge. Before being born into this world it sinks down, losing its wings and surrendering to amnesia.[2] If later in life we are to recapture our true wisdom we must do so by recalling some glimpse of our original pristine state, a process of remembering (*anamnesis*) rather than acquiring.

While this story seems fanciful—it is unlikely that Plato himself took it literally—there is small doubt that we are born into this world with little memory of what came before and evidently little ability to form new long-lasting memories for the first two or three years of life. Nevertheless, most experts agree that the neonate is becoming conscious by the end of the second trimester of pregnancy,[3] and few would argue that a healthy newborn is not equipped with consciousness. Indeed, those who have had the experience of holding a newborn and seeing the infant quisitively peering into their eyes can hardly doubt that someone is home.

Perhaps it is not news that our understanding of the world in which we live changes as we grow from infancy to childhood and on to adulthood. This change, in all the gradations it entails, gives our experience a palpable developmental dimension. In fact, developmental changes are seen in all four quadrants. As we grow mentally our bodies grow too, as do the kinds of relationships we have with others. Our sense of community transforms from the first infantile union with our parents, especially our mother, to an emerging awareness of ourselves as individuals, and then on to an understanding of our place in the larger communities of which we take part. These communities include our extended families, our colleagues at work, our spiritual companions, and so on. Thus, we can track the path of growth in all four quadrants, seeing that each is correlated with the others.

Remembering childhood

Here are some recollections of earliest memories:

> I remember just laying on the ground looking up at the sky, and back then I thought that it was a huge ocean with the clouds being fog and the sun being a large light bulb that was turned on during the day so that we could see the world. When the wind came by, I would then pretend that I was just flying above this ocean.

> I was in my crib, in my room at night. I looked down and saw the big tail of the alligator who lived underneath it. It was black and curled outward slowly so I could see it from the bars of the crib. It startled me at first, but I saw him many times after that and got used to him being there. He would only show up at night, and I would see his tail and feet sometimes moving around. He didn't scare me. He was like a silent, nighttime friend.

Thinking my dead cat that we buried in the backyard was going to grow into a tree with kittens on it.

Eating a worm.

Around age 3, I suddenly became conscious that I was sitting at the kitchen table one afternoon, gazing at the wallpaper. It was very quiet. What I saw was familiar—I knew I'd seen it many times—but I felt like I was emerging from a dream and have no recollection of my life prior to that.[4]

Can you recall an idea or event from childhood that makes no sense to you today? I remember playing in a backyard sand pile after a heavy summer rain. I kept a big Maxwell House coffee can there for important operations involving sand. On this particular morning it was filled with water. For some reason I started pouring sand into it and to my astonishment water started flowing over the rim. I came to the realization that pouring sand into a can of water creates more water!

As a young child certain phrases left me baffled. For instance, my grandmother said, "If it's not in your head it's in your heels!" Hmm... When somewhat older but still a child I was confused by the adage, "A stitch in time saves nine." This little motto is particularly instructive. Apparently by late childhood I was mentally advanced enough to think of time in a kind of Newtonian way, as something with extension, but I was puzzled by the idea of putting stitches into it. I now realize that it was precisely this literal approach that caused my confusion. The adage is an allegory, not a description of real events. It is not meant to be taken literally any more than the aphorism, "A bird in the hand is worth two in the bush," (another one I had trouble with), should be taken as advice about birds and bushes.

There is a movement in mental growth from pure fantasy during infancy and early childhood, as illustrated in the examples above, to literalism in more mature childhood, and then on to the abstract thinking of adults. To a young child the phrase "old wine in new bottles"[5] may call up images of wine and bottles (if the child is familiar with wine and bottles), but a more mature child will most likely think it has something to do with rebottling wine. Only the adult mind understands this phrase in terms of the abstract notion of telling old facts or stories in new words.

Recalling events from childhood reminds us that the world seemed different to us then than it does now. Besides differences in understanding, illustrated by the adages above, the world of childhood is brighter, more colorful, and more intense than the world of the adult. Time and space are different too. For example, for many Christian children it takes an amazing number of long slow weeks to get from Thanksgiving to Christmas and Santa Claus. No wonder the White Witch in C.S. Lewis' *The Lion, the Witch, and the Wardrobe* could arrange for it to always be winter but never to be Christmas.

The truth is that we all have lived in several worlds and have been a number of different people by the time we have grown up, each representing a different stage of development. This fact is easier to see when we observe our children than when we sift through personal memories because these differences are easier to observe from the outside than the inside. In Wilber's words,

> One of the major difficulties in coming to terms with a *stage conception* is that most people, even if they are in fact progressing through stages of competence, *rarely experience anything that feels or looks like a stage.* In their own direct experience, "stages" make no sense at all... We spot them only by standing back from unreflective experience, comparing our experiences with others, and seeing if there are any common patterns. If these common patterns check out in numerous different settings, then we are justified in assuming that various stages are involved. But in all cases, these stages are the product of direct investigation and research, not abstract philosophizing.[6]

There are informal names for the major stages children pass through as they mature. First after birth comes infancy, then the toddler stage followed by young childhood, say, three to six years of age, after which follows what I like to call "adult childhood." This begins at around seven or eight years of age and continues to puberty at ten or twelve. In many ways children in this stage are complete little people. Many stories are written about them because they are surprisingly intelligent and mature, and they are capable of a single-minded purposefulness. From *Harry Potter* to *The Lord of the Flies*, such stories deal with the lives and adventures of children who seem very much like adults in their emotional and intellectual maturity. Following this period of late childhood comes adolescence with its social and hormonal upheavals, near the end of which we stumble into young adulthood.

The above overview of growth stages is very informal of course, but characterizes the developmental stages every parent sees and all of us once experienced first-hand if we could only remember what it was like to have been there.

Jean Piaget and the magical world of the child

We can improve our understanding of these stages of development by taking advantage of the investigations of psychologists who have labored to discover how children grow. For instance, during the middle decades of the twentieth century the Swiss researcher Jean Piaget made great contributions to our understanding of the mind of the child. Though there have since been many refinements to his work, the basic model he created remains the cornerstone of developmental psychology even today.

At the core of Piaget's thinking is the concept of *schemas* (or *schemata*). In its original Greek meaning a *schema* is literally a shape or a plan. The idea is best translated into modern English as a *pattern*, in this case of thought or behavior. Most infant learning comes in the form of new physical skills such as grasping, crawling, standing, and walking. Each involves a pattern of body movement. These can be thought of as schemas. For example, there is a schema for grasping, a schema for crawling, a schema for standing, and so on. The more complex the behavior the more likely it will become coordinated with perceptual schemas involving vision as well as balance and touch.

Grasping is very simple, but walking is more complex. During the first two years after birth the infant acquires a variety of increasingly complex schemas. Meanwhile, near the end of the first year infants begin to use simple words like "cat" and "doggie." By the end of the second year they are making short sentences such as, "Me go home." These initial sentences are word patterns, or linguistic schemas, which will grow enormously in intricacy during the coming years.

While the first two years of life, which Piaget termed the *Sensory-Motor Period*, are mostly dedicated to mastering one's own body and learning to move around in the world, later learning is more concerned with understanding the world. Thus begins a slow shift towards internal or conceptual learning that will involve many stages of development. By the time we become adults almost all of our learning arrives in the form of new ideas, facts, and concepts. Of course we can always learn new physical skills as well, such as dancing, drawing, or playing golf, but for most of us, most of the time, the lion's share of our learning takes place right in our heads.

I sometimes think of mental schemas as lines of code in a computer program. Each line is a simple instruction to the computer such as "Add 2 to X then divide the sum by 3" (where X is a number the user enters from the keypad), or "If the number the user enters is greater then 12 then return to the first line and start over." When enough of these steps are executed in sequence the result is a complex program. Now consider how this is similar to mental reasoning. For instance, let us examine how a child learns basic arithmetic.

Even before the child can learn much about arithmetic he or she has to master some form of "number concept." This is a fairly basic schema. For instance, if I hold up my hand with all my fingers flared out the child must be able to understand "5." Just two fingers must be understood to signal "2" and so on. This is pretty basic stuff but necessary in order to get on with the more sophisticated business of counting. Counting involves the placement of numbers in sequence, "1, 2, 3..." So the ability to count is a schema that depends on, and actually incorporates, the more basic schema of numbers.

Now we're cooking!

The next level of sophistication is to count by leaps and bounds; that is, to learn how to add. So, 4 plus 4 is counting "1, 2, 3, 4" and "5, 6, 7, 8" – or 8! Most of us start by doing this on our fingers. In fact, finger counting is a perfect example of a behavioral pattern or schema that later moves into our heads as an internal schema we can enact without fingers. But it is still a schema, much like a computer program.

Now, it is a proven fact that if a child is taught to parrot correct addition by rote memorization he or she will have no idea how to use this knowledge in the real world. For instance, given two paper bags, one with three apples in it and one with four, the child will not be able to tell you the total number of apples. It is essential that schemas be built from the ground up as complex structures, or in this case that the child be familiar with counting before trying to understand addition.

To take this line of reasoning one step further, let's briefly consider how a child learns to multiply. Reflection will tell us that multiplication is just adding by leaps and bounds, not unlike the way adding is counting by leaps and bounds. So 4 times 4 is really 4 + 4 + 4 + 4, giving us 16. Here again, if the child does not understand the previous step, in this case addition, he or she can memorize multiplication tables until blue in the face but will never understand multiplication.

Notice something important here. Each level of achievement, each new and more sophisticated schema, is built from the schemas below it. It is a bit like building a house. Each floor rests on the one below, except that in the house of mathematics each is actually made out of the floor beneath, all the way down and all the way up. Now we come to another important point: *no step can be omitted or passed over*. In other words, you cannot build a house starting with the second or third floor while the space below remains empty air. Likewise, no one can leapfrog to advanced levels of growth without first mastering the earlier elementary levels. We have here a central principle of mental development and, indeed, of psychological development in general. No step or stage can be omitted. Each must be experienced and absorbed completely before moving on. This goes for virtually all types of development, whether we are learning mathematics or formal logic, moral reasoning or jurisprudence, artistic or musical skills, and so on. One must acquire the basic concepts, or schemas, and from them develop more complex and supple schemas. This is what education is all about. It is not about the acquisition of facts to be regurgitated on a test, but the ability to manipulate complex concepts in order to understand and even explore complex situations and new possibilities. This is why only lower level college courses rely on multiple-choice tests while advanced ones typically require independent thinking and concept development expressed in essays and papers.

But hold on. Let's not forget that our primary interest is in the experiential worlds through which childhood carries us. The important point here is that *we experience these worlds because they are patterned for us by our own inner schemas.* Piaget divided childhood into four "periods," or stages. These are briefly introduced below because they are the starting points for understanding much of the discussion of child and adult development that will follow. With these in mind, we can see how childhood experiences of the self and the world change as we grow. Later we will explore the strange idea that the growth and development of every child mirrors the much longer developmental history of human consciousness.

Sensorimotor Period (birth to about age 2)

These age estimates represent only a rough approximation of the average time most children spend in each period. Some children move through the stages more quickly and others more slowly. The sensorimotor period is the first developmental stage and is named for the fact that children are primarily involved in acquiring basic sensory and motor skills such as crawling, standing, walking, and grasping, and coordinating these with vision, hearing, and so on. For instance, newborns can do little with their hands, but midway through the first year they begin to develop hand-eye coordination that allows them to grasp objects that are seen.[7] In six to nine months they begin to sit up unaided, and by the end of the first year they are standing up on their own and taking their first steps.

By six to nine months an infant is babbling. During this time they produce virtually all the sounds of every human language. But as they learn to speak during their second year this range is reduced and with it their ability to discriminate certain sounds. For instance, typical American and English infants can no longer discriminate certain sounds important in Japanese and to North West Coast Native Americans. In one's own language, however, new words are acquired readily. A two-year-old knows about 50 words, but can understand more in context. By the end of the second year, most children are chattering away.

During these first two years dramatic changes are taking place in the infant's inner life as well. Most theorists agree with William James' characterization of the experiential world of the newborn as a "big blooming buzzing confusion."[8] Perhaps we should just say "blooming and buzzing" because the infant has no conceptual schemas yet, so no thoughts are percolating that could give rise to confusion. It is more a matter of being submerged in the stream of experience with nothing between the infant and the flickering sensory images of the world. At this point the infant is making no distinction between itself and the world around. It is still submerged in an innocent and, if the infant is well cared for, paradisiacal unity with a world that provides for all its basic needs. In Wilber's words, "The neonate's awareness is spaceless, timeless, objectless (but not eventless)."[9]

During the second half of his or her first year of life the infant begins to differentiate from the mother or primary caretaker in a *physical* sense, gaining the first awareness of its own body as separate from the mother's body and surroundings.[10] In the second year he or she begins to acquire a separate sense of an *emotional* self as well. At this point the child is still a creature of impulse and emotion, and his or her identity is still very much rooted in the mother, but already the beginnings of individual identity and self-awareness are starting to bloom. Concepts (schemas) of space and time are still indefinite and the basic schema for causality—i.e., understanding that one thing can cause another—is just emerging.

The second year of life will see the psychological emergence of the infant, now with an embryonic but distinct emotional and verbal self that is separate from the mother. It is during this year that the infant's inner life is transforming rapidly from one of undifferentiated impulse and emotion to that of a child with his or her own sense of self, though still very much under the sway of drives and emotions, as every parent knows. At this age the world of the child is "egocentric," that is, the child sees everything from his or her own point of view, even to the extent of being "perceptually bound." The latter means that a child cannot imagine what it is like to see things from somewhere else, such as from the other side of the room, even if he or she just returned from there. Needless to say, it is pointless to lecture a two-year-old child on what it feels like to be someone else—for example a tired mother or hurt friend. Moreover, the young person still has a considerable distance to travel before developing any sort of self-awareness in the "strong sense," that is, capable of actually reflecting on what it is like to be oneself and to be alive.[11]

Preoperational Period (2 to about 7)

This is sometimes called the "play period" for obvious reasons. Young mammals of virtually every kind, from cats, to whales, to human children, fill every opportunity with play. In doing so they stretch and exercise their growing bodies, along the way acquiring physical agility and social skills later essential to their adult lives.

During this period children begin to acquire many mental schemas so basic to understanding reality that as adults it is difficult to imagine living without them. They include the earliest intuitions about space, time, and causality, though children do not yet entertain conscious thoughts about these. Their world is still egocentric, or centered about themselves, and through most of this period children are unable to sort objects or ideas according to more than one aspect at a time. For example, suppose a preoperational child is shown a pasture where four horses and three cows can be seen. If the child is then asked, "Are there more horses or animals?" he or she will answer, "There are more horses. See, there are four horses and only three cows!"

Similarly, through most of this period the child does not have a clear schema for *conservation*, that is, an understanding that objects are stable and don't change in volume or amount, or even appear or disappear out of nowhere. For instance, you can show a five-year-old boy two large glasses of orange juice filled to the same level. If you pour the contents of one glass into a wide beaker or pie pan, he will now tell you there is less juice in the pie pan than there is in the remaining glass. ("See, the glass is filled up higher than the pan.") Pouring the juice from the pan back into the original glass, however, restores the equivalence of volume. The child sees no contradiction in this and you can do it all day if you like without creating confusion or surprise. Similar "Piagetian tasks" can be done with clay and marbles. The child will report fewer marbles when they are poured into the pie pan, and less clay when it is squashed down from the shape of a ball into a wide flat pancake.

It is not difficult to understand that the preoperational child is often given to magical thinking, which is another way of saying they live in a magical world. Such thinking confuses fantasy with objective reality. If you ask a four-year-old why it rains, he or she may tell you it is so that the flowers can grow and blossom. Physical objects such as dolls and other toys can have lives of their own. Imaginary playmates are not uncommon during this period. Moreover, children at this stage often blame themselves for events that are not of their own doing. A three-year-old boy might tell you he hurt his knee because he was playing in the front yard where his mommy told him not to go, rather than because he tripped on a stone. Tragically, children often blame themselves for parental conflicts in which they played no part whatsoever.

Concrete Operations Period (7 to about 12)

As soon as the child matures to this stage of intellectual development, he may reply to the orange juice in the pie pan problem the same way my own seven-year-old nephew did. He said, "You can't fool me! If you pour that milk back into the tall glass it will be the same amount as it was before." He was taking advantage of a newly acquired schema of *reversibility*, which allowed him to run the whole thing backwards in his mind's eye, as it were, and see that he would again obtain the original volume of milk, all of which helped anchor the newly acquired conservation schema mentioned above. During the Concrete Operations Period children acquire many such schemas essential to adult intelligence in the Formal Operations period to follow. To list and discuss them all would take us far off track, but they are described in many resources on the growth of intelligence in the child.[12]

The Concrete Operations Period is all about understanding symbols and following rules—rules of logic, rules of language, and rules of behavior. This being the case, children in this period can seem remarkably intelligent. They play complex games such as checkers, baseball, and Monopoly, but they always do so according to pre-given rules that are not questioned. They quickly learn basic arithmetic and can perform complex classification tasks that require "multiple classification" skills such as recognizing that both horses and cows are included in the class of mammals, and that mammals are included in the larger class of animals.

Though it may seem during this stage that children act and think like adults there is an important difference. The mental achievements of Concrete Operations are limited by the fact that they must always deal in concrete objects and events. Young people in this stage do not think in terms of abstractions. See-through mechanical models, for example, are excellent for teaching science at this stage, and if the teacher does not actually have physical objects such as marbles, bananas, or mechanical models, then he or she needs to talk about concrete objects and situations. It is only later, when young persons achieve the next stage, termed Formal Operations, that they will be capable of abstract thought. For example, efforts have been made to extend school debating contests down to this age range, as is done with spelling bees. The results of such efforts, however, have been disastrous. While spelling is based on rules and factual knowledge about concrete words (symbols), debates concern principles such as morality and justice. These highly abstract concepts are well beyond the grasp of Concrete Operations children. Indeed, as we will see in the next chapter, they are beyond the scope of many adults as well.

Formal Operations (12 years and over)

As mentioned previously, Piaget referred to the final stage of the intellectual growth of young persons as Formal Operations, indicating that he or she can now think in "formal" or abstract terms without needing to rely on ideas of concrete objects for examples. Instead of depending on apples and oranges to teach arithmetic, and even without imagining the presence of apples or oranges, the Formal Operations thinker can understand abstract relationships expressed, for instance, in equations such as,

$$X = 3Y + Z$$

Such a relationship might apply to any number of situations, and the variables (X, Y, and Z) can represent anything from lemons to foot-pounds.

In fact, Formal Operations opens the door to advanced thinking of many kinds. Legal reasoning, for instance, relies on notions of equality, justice, and consistency over a wide range of actual situations, as does mature political reasoning. Indeed, the ability to reason in terms of broad generalizations is vital to all forms of science and scholarship, and to the arts as well. It is an essential tool of adult intelligence.

Having acquired skills in formal operations thinking, the young person may, for the first time, be able to stand outside himself or herself as an objective observer. This act can trigger memorable experiences of awakening as a human being, sometimes eliciting palpable transcendent overtones. A beautiful example of such an awakening was described by Richard Hughes in his 1928 book, *A High Wind in Jamaica: The Innocent Voyage*. It happened to Emily, who had been experiencing weeks of aimless activity while aboard a pirate ship when one day she suddenly realized who she was.

> …She had been playing houses in a nook right in the bows… thinking vaguely about some bees and a fairy queen, when it suddenly flashed into her mind that she was *she*.
>
> She stopped dead, and began looking over all of her person which came within the range of her eyes. She could not see much, except a fore-shortened view of the front of her frock, and her hands when she lifted them for inspection; but it was enough for her to form a rough idea of the little body she suddenly realized to be hers.
>
> She began to laugh, rather mockingly. "Well!" she thought, in effect. "Fancy *you*, of all people, going and getting caught like this!—You can't get out of it now, not for a very long time: you'll have to go through with being a child, and growing up, and getting old, before you'll be quit of this mad prank!"[13]

And now we too will move on to the next chapter and to adulthood.

5. The Adult Mind—Lines

Passage into the logical or discursive period brings with it three very striking and fruitful gains. First, language develops pari passu with generalization, and gives to all the cognitive and emotional processes the adequate instrument of expression and of personal intercourse. Secondly, the sense of self passes, along with other contents, through various phases of growth, and becomes the "ego" over against the social "alter"... And, thirdly, the rise of judgment brings in reflection, the turning-in of the thinker upon his own mental processes. With reflection, the thinker and agent becomes the judge, the critic, the interpreter, the philosopher.

—James Mark Baldwin, 1930 [1]

The above passage, written early in the twentieth century by one of the founding fathers of American psychology, expresses the importance of the growth and development of the intellect for the cultivation of a mature sense of *self*. According to *integral psychology* [2] the self is one of many facets, or *lines*, of psychological growth. In this chapter we will examine some of these facets, beginning with the self line. But first let us become more familiar with the general idea of developmental lines.

Lines of Development

Lines refer to specific skills, traits, or areas of knowledge that we acquire as we grow from childhood into adulthood. In contrast to the notion of lines, most early researchers such as Jean Piaget and James Mark Baldwin tended to think of mental development as traveling a single broad path toward maturation. This reasoning implied that once a young person was capable of applying formal operations thinking to mathematics he or she was also likely to be capable of applying it to other fields as well, for example, politics, art, ethics, and so on. [3] Perhaps not surprisingly it turns out this is not the case.

The discovery that different skills such as mathematical reasoning, artistic judgment, ethical reasoning, and social adeptness mature at different rates became widely recognized for the first time in the 1970s. Curiously enough this came about through efforts on the part of the artificial intelligence community to create computer programs capable of producing ordinary person-like behaviors in robots. A well-known program named SHRDLU was written by Terry Winograd at MIT to perform a variety of simple but realistic tasks such as stacking boxes of different sizes and colors or placing certain containers inside each other.[4] These operations were carried out in an imaginary world space containing only plain geometric objects. To everyone's amazement, however, these seemingly uncomplicated tasks turned out to be much more difficult than expected. It seems that people take many facts about the world for granted that computers don't know. Programs designed to perform simple simulations of life in the real world regularly made jaw-droppingly stupid mistakes. Characters walked through walls instead of doors, sat on floors instead of chairs, and so on. These sorts of seemingly ridiculous actions make perfect sense when you realize that the computer, not having grown up in the real world, did not know even simple rules about the material world. SHRDLU had to learn that it couldn't move objects through walls or other solid matter, that such objects will rest on top of each other, etc. Human beings learn these facts as elementary schemas during the fist year or two of life, but for computers they are big news. As it turns out knowledge, as well as skill, is *information intensive*. A great deal of information goes into even the simplest real world activities.

What this means in plain English is that skills rely heavily on experience. We all know this if we stop to think about it. If you want a child to become an accomplished violinist you start them out playing the violin as early as possible. If you want to produce a dancer you start the child dancing as early as you can. The accumulation of experience, and the facts and schemas that come with it, are what make the difference between a modestly skilled performer and a master.

This generalization is especially apparent in fields that rely on detailed knowledge. A few years back a graduate student at the University of Chicago was talking with her six-year-old daughter about one of the child's favorite topics, dinosaurs. When she asked her daughter about different kinds of dinosaurs, the latter effortlessly produced an impressive list for her mother; there were terrestrial dinosaurs, arboreal dinosaurs, aquatic dinosaurs, herbivores, carnivores, and omnivores, nocturnal dinosaurs, diurnal dinosaurs, crepuscular dinosaurs; and so on! She not only knew all these different categories of dinosaurs, but she could converse about them in full formal operations mode. How was this possible? In short, it was possible because the child had spent so much time thinking about and learning everything she could find concerning dinosaurs! Strangely, though, when the topic turned to dogs, cooking, art, morals, geography, or arithmetic, she again became a six-year-old. Her special knowledge applied to dinosaurs alone. With this in mind, it is perhaps not too surprising that children sometimes make better ethical judgments about pets than about people. They often have had more experience taking care of pets.

Getting back to lines, the point of all this is that we become skilled, knowledgeable, and competent in those areas in which we have the most experience. Of course I understand that this is not the entire story. Genetics certainly plays an important role, though scientists have a long way to go before they will know exactly how much. But the lion's share of developmental influence nevertheless comes right out of the richness of our own experiences as we grow and mature. And this is a process that continues during our entire lives.

The above in mind, it is perhaps not surprising that each of us exhibits our own unique pattern of talents and skills. These can be represented in a *psychograph* such as that shown in Figure 5.1.

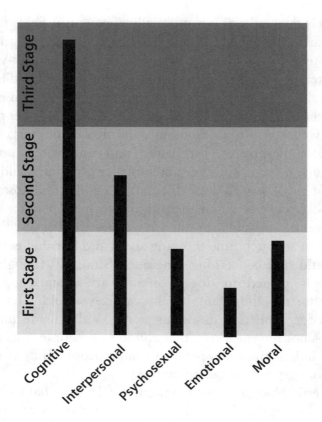

Figure 5.1. A Simple Psychograph[5]

Here we see the profile of an individual who has strong intellectual, or cognitive, development, but whose interpersonal skills are relatively modest, and whose psychosexual, emotional, and moral lines are even less mature. We are looking at an intellectually impressive person with the emotional development of a child and interpersonal skills that are average at best. I would not recommend becoming emotionally involved with this person.

Psychographs can be drawn to include any developmental dimension you like. For instance, Figure 5.2 shows a different psychograph that includes lines for cognitive as well as spiritual development, aesthetic judgment, moral reasoning, emotional maturity, and kinesthic ability.

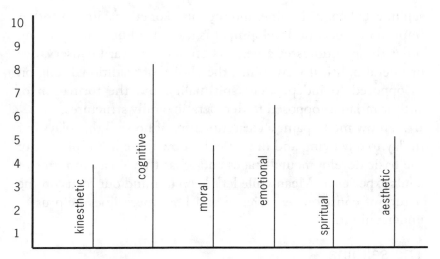

Figure 5.2. A different psychograph [6]

Not just children

The big news, which you have no doubt already figured out, is that we are not just talking about children and adolescents here. The plain fact is that many people do not develop all of their lines to the formal operations level, or even anywhere near it. Due to the limiting effects of poor family upbringing, disadvantaged education, restrictive religious training and other shortcomings for growth and development, many of us arrive at adulthood with some or all of our lines short of formal operations.

What all this discloses about everyday life is that we are each constantly surrounded by an amazing variety of people who see the world through different developmental lenses than ourselves, and different than each other. Given the large number of developmental lines—the exact figure is not known—and allowing for the fact that we are all deeply influenced by our own cultural backgrounds and unique personal histories, this translates into a staggering level of diversity. As a society we are coming to understand the importance of cultural diversity but we have not yet begun to recognize the importance of developmental diversity. Among the most important lines in this regard are the self line, the cognitive line, and the moral or ethical line. Another important aspect of development is the value line which, among other things, addresses a person's tendency toward conservative or liberal political viewpoints, the choice of traditional religion as opposed to independent spirituality, and the formation of authoritarian as opposed to democratic family structures.

Allow me to paint a clearer picture of how all this plays out in day to day living and in particular how these lines spin out of the basic developmental stages and what they mean in terms of adult experience. Meanwhile let's keep in mind our focus on the nature of conscious experience and how these lines help us to understand it.

The self line

The self line is especially important because it represents what we ordinarily think of as personal growth and development in a psychological sense. Let's start with basic the idea of the *self*. Carl Rogers, one of the founders of humanistic psychology, defined the self very simply as all the perceptions a person has about him or herself. This is an experiential definition that captures the essence of the idea of the self very nicely. Thus, we can think of the self as the subjective core of our conscious personality, the facet of ourselves most clearly identified with what we mean by "I" or "me." When thinking about growth and development, however, we need to look more deeply into the self and realize that it is in fact more than our conscious sense of who we are. Indeed, it is an entire psychological structure which, in Wilber's words, acts as "the locus of identification, volition, defense, organization, and 'metabolism' ('digestion' of experiences at each level of structural growth and development)."[7] In other words, the self is a kind of self-organizing vortex at the center of the personality that sorts, organizes, and responds to the experiences the world brings us.

The self line passes through several stages of development on the way to adulthood. These correspond to and in many ways are created by the underlying schemas that form the developmental stages first mapped by Piaget and explored in the proceeding chapter.

There is every reason to suspect that the newborn infant has no sense of self, or for that matter any kind of feeling of the sense of separate identity that we take for granted as adults. "Primary" schemas such as suckling, grasping, and tracking objects visually have not yet organized themselves into complex behavior, let alone complex internal mental processes. Thus the newborn lives in a pure stream of experience, undergirded by a basic drive for food and undifferentiated feelings of happiness and unhappiness.[8]

Around the end of the first year of life the infant begins to acquire language, but is still far from manipulating words as symbols in ways that lead to logical thinking. During the preoperational period of roughly two to six years the child acquires the ability to distinguish objects and other people as separate from him or herself, but is largely submerged in his or her own feelings and perspectives. That is to say, the world is taken for granted just the way the child sees and feels it to be. For example, if a child in this period likes you, you are nice; if he or she does not like you, you are mean. Indeed, young people don't outgrow this self-centered view entirely until they reach adulthood, if they are fortunate enough to outgrow it at all.

For two to six-year-old children this is all very literal. Toys such as dolls and teddy bears have inner lives of their own, and material objects can be mean or kind, just like people. Without a clear sense of separation between inner and outer reality children are engulfed in and driven by their feelings and impulses. This in mind, it is perhaps not surprising that preoperational children do not engage in moral reasoning, but rather tend to act in terms of rewards and punishments. Meanwhile they live in a richly imaginative universe that may include talking animals and fairies as well as the scary creatures that live in the darkness under the bed. Indeed, it is a rare child living in an old house who would venture into the attic alone, even in the daytime.[9]

The preoperational child does not have a developed sense

of space, time, or causality, all of which require advanced adult mental schemas. This fact, combined with an inability to clearly distinguish inner from outer realities affords rich ground for magical thinking. Thus events in the external world take on the coloration of the child's own feelings and appear frightening, wondrous, judgmental, and so on. It is as if the Freudian defense mechanism of projection operates in a fluid and unconstrained fashion on children in this age range.

Now, let me point out yet again that these descriptions are not simply psychological accounts of child development. They sketch the dimensions of the experiential worlds of the child. They also map the qualities of the experience of adults who have, one way or another, failed to develop a mature sense of self. Such adults continue to experience the world in ways similar to children.

Around six or seven years of age, earlier for some, the child makes a significant transition into Piaget's concrete operations period. With this change he or she begins to behave in many ways much like an adult and, indeed, in terms of the lines for the self and for moral reasoning, many adults never grow past this stage. Youth at the concrete operations stage can for the first time appreciate another person's point of view, but they still cannot do so while keeping their own or a third party's perspective in mind. Hence, they can understand and empathize with another, but cannot navigate complex social relationships. We see this even in young teenagers, who will take sides in virtually every dispute and who cannot seem to see the other person's perspective while holding onto their own. As many readers know from personal experience, trying to explain a complicated social situation to an argumentative teenager is like trying to whistle in the wind.

During the concrete operations period language becomes very important, particularly in the sense that children accept linguistic rules almost without question. As noted in the previous chapter such children regard game and play rules given to them by an authority such as a parent, or a teacher, to be absolute and beyond question. The child's sense of self follows in the same vein. While younger children answer the question, "What or where is your self?" by pointing to their physical body, at the concrete operations stage they speak in terms of social roles such as being a student at a particular school, belonging to a soccer team or church, being a member of a particular family, and so on.[10] The young person is said to have a social *persona* (from the Greek meaning *mask*) that defines the self. Many adults have a similar sense of who they are. For instance, they identify with a family, team, church, or tribe. I once experienced an extreme version of this in a thirty-something college student who introduced herself as "Mrs. Blackburn." Even during informal group discussions, and in the face of efforts by others, including myself, to encourage her to participate under her own first name, she continued to insist that she was none other than "Mrs. Blackburn!"[11]

It is perhaps not surprising that concrete operations children—and adults—tend to see other people in terms of social stereotypes and make moral as well as value judgments based on peer group consensus. For these reasons this phase of development is often referred to as the "conformity" period. In terms of social behavior the tendency toward conformity often continues right through adolescence and on into the mid or even late teens, during which time youth often feel compelled to adopt the values and styles of their same-age peers. This is not news to anyone.

Paradoxically, in contrast to the tendency toward conformity, young people in the late concrete operations period—now becoming adolescents—often shift away from conformity in their ethical thinking in favor of an increasing belief in absolute morality. At this point youths tend to believe there is a true and final solution to any moral question. Moral dilemmas are more about *finding* this solution than seeking some personal advantage as in previous developmental stages, or balancing positive and negative aspects of the situation as will come in later ones.

Many adults retain this absolute morality style of thinking throughout their lives, as many remain at the earlier conformist stage. The absolute view of morality is characteristic of many conservative religions and would seem to be the root of fundamentalism in all its many forms, an apparent fact that was pointed out decades ago by pioneering morality researcher Lawrence Kohlberg. His prominent student, Carol Gilligan disagreed, however, arguing that fundamentalism is actually powered by conformity and hence represents an even lower level of development. Eventually the research data, and Kohlberg himself, came to support this view. This is an important observation because it tells us that for a fundamentalist any convincing "argument" has more to do with group opinion and expectations than logical or factual reasoning. On a more optimistic note, Kohlberg discovered that each of us is capable of understanding and becoming attracted to the moral stage just beyond the one that dominates our own behavior. This in mind, it is possible to appeal to a fundamentalist on the basis of *authority*, for example by showing that it is against the teachings of the Bible or Koran to kill or injure other human beings.

According to Piaget somewhere around 12 years of age, though I suspect younger for many contemporary youth,[12] comes the onset of adult intelligence, which he termed formal operations. The phrase itself implies an ability to think in abstractions, seeking general rules and principles while creating and testing hypotheses about the nature of reality. This is a "scientific" orientation that relies on logic and empirical observation for its answers. It is the dominant intellectual style among educated adults throughout the contemporary world, though it does not represent the actual majority of people, especially in countries where only small numbers are fortunate enough to receive advanced educations. Formal operations thinking often yields a no-nonsense point of view that relies on science and cost-effective finances to get along in a dog-eat-dog world, rather than on conformity to social roles, mythic beliefs, or tribal magic. Indeed, its greatest weakness lies in the rejection of these earlier ways of finding personal meaning, leaving concrete operations persons to fend for themselves with reason alone to seek purpose in a harsh world.

Another aspect of the formal operations stage is a significant maturation of the ego. Unfortunately, the term *"ego"* can be confusing because it is used in so many ways. Freud's original use of the word was taken directly from the Latin, meaning "I myself." With this in mind it is easy to see how it is often used interchangeably with the word *self.* But Freud and other theorists from Carl Jung to modern psychiatrists and psychologists have consistently associated ego with what Freud termed *the reality principle.* The latter refers to the many ways we manage our affairs to effectively meet the demands of reality or, in plain English, how we cope with the world around us. This process begins very early in childhood as the infant learns to withhold the immediate satisfaction of basic biological urges such as the need to defecate, as well as eating and drinking, in each case for the benefit of future satisfaction at appropriate times and places. As we grow we learn to put off all kinds of rewards until the appropriate setting is found. All this is basic psychoanalytic theory, but my point is that when we speak of the ego we are speaking in terms of how an individual copes, either effectively or ineffectively, with reality. The development of this ability to cope with reality does not make impressive progress until concrete operations thinking is established. This in mind, it is appropriate to identify the ego more plainly with adolescent and especially adult levels of development than with childhood, even though the roots of ego growth start very early with the first withholding of immediate pleasure for later and more appropriate satisfaction.

The word *ego* is often used in common parlance to refer to an individual's sense of self-confidence, self-importance, or even self-aggrandizement. A person who displays an excess of these traits is said to have a "big ego." It is easy to see how this notion of the ego dovetails with the traditional definition of the ego as the reality principle. A person with a "big ego" seems indeed to be working overtime to manage reality, manipulating not only material objects in their environment but other people who have the unfortunate luck of being near them. It is also easy to see how the term *ego* is equated with the term *self,* since both have to do with how we see and experience ourselves. The word *ego*, however, puts special emphasis on how we deal realistically with the objective world in which we live, while *self* makes reference specifically to our sense of who we are, for example as used in the phrase *self-concept*. It is worth noting that the deep structure of the self actually includes those aspects of the ego that organize our realistic exchanges with the objective world. In other words, at a deeper psychological level, the two concepts overlap.

It is not uncommon for theorists such as Jane Loevinger to speak of ego development from infancy.[13] In doing so they are usually referring to how infants and children relate to the outside world. Examples include responding to rewards and punishments, seeking conformity, and so on—exactly what we have already seen. The fact is, however, that it is not until a young person approaches formal operations that he or she actually has a complete and adequate working ego in place. Prior to formal operations the ability to cope realistically with the objective world through clear and logical thinking has not yet replaced the thinking styles of childhood.

The world maker or the cognitive line

It will come as no surprise that the cognitive line is essential to the self line, setting the tone and substance for the growth and maturation of the self.[14] If we drew a separate line for the ego it would be vital to that as well. Indeed, the mental abilities that decide the way we approach our day to day challenges, how we relate to others, and how we navigate the complexities of our daily lives all rest on the sufficiency and maturity of our cognitive line. As we have seen, much of the growth and maturation of the self and the ego depend directly on the development of the mental capacities represented by this line.

All this is because we make sense out of experiences, including experiences of ourselves, according to the maturity of our intelligence. For example, a preoperational child is unable to separate fantasy from sensory impressions, and therefore lives in a world of animated toys and imaginary playmates. On the other hand, the concrete operational child is good at recognizing objective reality for what it is, but is unable to see it in broader contexts that allow generalizations. As we have seen, this child tends to follow rules slavishly and sees morality in terms of conformity, and later in terms of absolute imperatives. Only the formal operations adolescent is able to understand the importance of generalizations, for example, in mathematics and ethics. Thus the adage, "What's good for the goose is good for the gander," makes sense to a formal operations adolescent, but not to the concrete operations child—or adult—who is too easily led into non-egalitarian and even fascist views of geese, and people as well. In such examples we see how effectively the cognitive line, which represents the way we understand the world, ourselves, and others, sets the stage for our moral and ethical views as well as our political persuasions. We can sum this all up by saying that the cognitive line sets the stage for how we see the world, how we perceive others and ourselves, and what ethical and moral positions we are likely to hold.

Many developmental lines

Before moving on let us note that there are many developmental lines. The actual number is unknown and will probably remain so for some time to come. But to get a sense of it Wilber suggests the following list in his book, *Integral Psychology*.[15]

1. The **cognitive line** (or awareness of what is).
2. The **moral line** (awareness of what should be).
3. The **emotional or affective line** (the full spectrum of emotions).
4. The **interpersonal line** (how I socially relate to others).
5. The **needs line** (such as Maslow's needs hierarchy).
6. The **self-identity line** (or "who am I?," such as Loevinger's ego development).
7. The **aesthetic line** (or the line of self-expression, beauty, art, and felt meaning).

8. The **psychosexual line**, which in its broadest sense means the entire spectrum of Eros (gross to subtle to causal).

9. The **spiritual line** (where "spirit" is viewed not just as Ground, and not just as the highest stage, but as its own line of unfolding).

10. The **values line** (or what a person considers most important, a line studied by Clare Graves and made popular by Spiral Dynamics).

In reality each of these can be further subdivided into threads that form developmental braids. For instance, the sophistication of a person's aesthetic taste may differ markedly between music, painting, sculpture, and dance. He or she may be an outstanding ballet dancer, but have little appreciation for modern art, to say nothing of other kinds of dance such as tap dancing or the tango. And there can be differences between active performance and passive appreciation. We might imagine that, in general, our level of accomplishment in any artistic endeavor roughly matches our level of sophistication as an observer, but this may not always be so. Human nature is paradoxical and full of surprises. A professor of literature, for instance, might be seen reading pulp fiction on weekends and a classical guitarist may enjoy jamming with a grunge rock band. The combinations are too varied to catalog.

Having briefly reviewed the stages of maturation from infancy up to adulthood, let's move on in the following chapters to an exploration of the nature of states and structures of consciousness, and then to an examination of growth beyond the ordinary.

6. States and Structures of Experience

> Suppose that an individual's experience...can be adequately described at any given moment if we know all the important dimensions along which experience varies and can assess the exact point along each dimension that an individual occupies... Each dimension may be the level of functioning of a psychological structure or process. We presume that we have a multidimensional map of psychological space and that by knowing exactly where the individual is in that psychological space we have adequately described his experiential reality for that given time.
>
> *—Charles Tart* [1]

Discussions about consciousness or experience are sometimes confusing because of the distinction between *states* and *structures*. If you toss the idea of *lines* into the mix, which you must do for a complete picture, the situation becomes even worse. So let's see what we can do to sort these three concepts out. We have already reviewed the notion of lines in the previous chapter, so here we continue with a description of states and then move on to structures.

States of consciousness

We are all familiar with states of consciousness [2] because we each experience several of them each day. They include waking, dreaming, and though we often do not remember, non-dream sleep as well. The differences between one and another of these states of consciousness is among the most profound and incontestable distinctions in nature, yet it is difficult to define precisely what makes each so distinct. Nonetheless they are different and we rarely confuse them. For instance, I have often asked groups of students if any of them would seriously consider the possibility that they were asleep and dreaming even as I spoke to them. So far out of hundreds of students I have had only one taker.

A survey of states of consciousness could occupy many pages. They include a wide range of chemically induced states, as well as meditative and trance states, hypnotic states, near death and out of the body experiences, dream states, and so on. And within each of these there are many variations. For example, dream experiences can come in a variety of different forms. In "lucid dreaming," for instance, the dreamer is aware of the fact that he or she is dreaming, and may even be able to exercise control over the events of the dream.[3] This, however, is not the only unique feature of lucid dreaming. Lucid dreams seem more intense and real than ordinary dreams, colors more brilliant, sounds clearer, and the dreamer more "awake" than in ordinary dreams. Another kind of dream, often referred to as "high dreams," revisits past psychedelic experiences once had using LSD or some other mind-altering substance.[4] A dream may also introduce the dreamer to some beatific experience that seems powerfully spiritual or even mystical. A few years ago such considerations led dream researcher Stanley Krippner and I to conclude that dreaming does not, in fact, represent a solitary state of consciousness, but is more like a doorway that opens into a variety of states.[5] For those interested in remarkable dream experiences, Krippner has even published an engaging little book titled *Extraordinary Dreams*. I note in passing that other forms of consciousness, such as meditative experiences, can also, like dreams, range widely both in terms of their richness, quality, and intensity.

Many states of consciousness have been described in detail,[6] but my goal here is simply to point out the wide range of such states. It is interesting to note that we are virtually never without some form of conscious experience. Indeed, we are conscious even during non-dream sleep when the mind flows with vague ruminations or is populated by dream-like images of lesser brilliance. It would seem that non-dream sleep is more a time of freely drifting forgetfulness than of no consciousness at all.

As long as we are alive it is doubtful that we are ever completely without consciousness.

Reflecting on the variety and wealth of states of consciousness, William James made the following now-famous observation.

> Our ordinary waking consciousness…is but one special type of consciousness, whilst all about it, parted from it by the filmiest of screens, there lie potential forms of consciousness entirely different. We may go through life without suspecting their existence; but apply the requisite stimulus, and at a touch they are there in all their completeness.[7]

Here I would like to point out the seemingly unimportant phrase at the end of the above quote: "..in all their completeness." It suggests the possibility that when one enters a state of consciousness one tends to enter it completely. This is not a point that James emphasized, but it turns out to be both true and important. An illustrative example is falling asleep. We can remain "half asleep" for short periods of time, but once we start down the slippery path to sleep we usually slide the whole way. This is why it is dangerous to drive when we are sleepy. Likewise, drug intoxication has a certain all-or-none, or at least off or on, quality to it. It is possible, of course, to be half intoxicated with alcohol or marijuana, for instance, but there is often a moment when one realizes that one is intoxicated—"stoned," "high," "tripping," whatever—and until that moment arrives the drug experience is not complete. On the other hand, when faced with an unexpected situation, say a phone call from one's mother, it is possible to return to something like ordinary consciousness surprisingly quickly.

How are states of consciousness organized?

In an effort to understand the dynamics of states of consciousness the leading consciousness theorist Charles Tart developed a systems theory of consciousness that illustrated why, when we enter a particular state of consciousness, the tendency is to enter it completely.[8] He reasoned that each state of consciousness is composed of a number of basic psychological processes such as memory, thought, sense of time, body-perception and the senses of hearing, smell, taste, and so on. For example, during marijuana intoxication the experience of sounds is accentuated, as is taste, while the body feels heavy and without energy. The result is that most, though not all, marijuana users tend to sit about listening to music—usually selections with a simple and pleasant rhythm—while endlessly munching on snacks. Short-term memory is weakened to the extent that, with sufficient intoxication, it becomes impossible to remember things well enough to complete a long sentence. Meanwhile, long-term memories of who we are and where we live are not greatly affected. Needless to say, this situation curtails any serious effort toward logical reasoning. Conversation tends to move in the direction of intuition and the imagination, often embellished with a great deal of giggling and laughter. In the meantime one's sense of time slows down so that five minutes may seem like an hour. People who try to drive while intoxicated run the risk of being stopped by the police for going too slow. Other drugs, such as LSD, however, have dramatically different effects. The latter heightens the visual sense, does not affect short-term memory, and potentially opens one to deep insights not accessed in ordinary everyday awareness. Often during LSD experiences people will spend time drawing, painting, or just looking around at other people and natural objects such as trees and flowers.

Tart's idea about states of consciousness was that the various psychological functions that come together to comprise a state—short and long term memory, the operation of the various sensory modes, sense of humor, the kind of "reasoning" that goes on in the state, etc.—fit together like pieces of a unique puzzle. One might say they form a kind of simpatico with each other, so that in any state of consciousness they all support each other, meanwhile tending to promote the continuation of the overall state. Thus, a state of consciousness is like one of those little convex metal disks the size of a quarter that were sold as Christmas toys when I was a child. Apply a little pressure to the center and you could pop them into a concaved configuration that would pop back in a few seconds, causing the disk to jump several feet into the air. A state of consciousness is like that, except it does not pop back so quickly, but only after the conditions that caused it have changed, e.g., after the drug has been metabolized, or one has had enough sleep.

The point in all this is that each state of consciousness has certain characteristics that work in synchrony to create the overall experience of that state. Stanley Krippner and I have explored the notion of states of consciousness in terms of modern theories of complexity.[9] The result is essentially the same. We viewed each state of consciousness as an *attractor*, which in chaos theory means a pattern of activity that a system—anything from a pendulum to a weather pattern, or in this case the mind and brain—is naturally drawn into by its own dynamics.

To expand on this idea a bit, we note that a pendulum tends to swing at a certain rate depending on its weight, the length of the shaft or cord that holds it, and so on. It is "attracted" to that rate by its own physics. Since the pendulum follows a predictable cyclic course time and time again, its highly reliable pattern of activity is characterized as a "cyclic attractor." A weather pattern, on the other hand, is much more complex but much more instructive as well. In any part of the world the weather tends to follow variable but familiar patterns from day to day, season to season, and year to year. The temperature is, for example, warm in the daytime and cool at night, hot in the summer and cold in the winter. It rains in the spring and is dry in the fall, and so on. The overall pattern is highly reliable on average, though it varies from instance to instance, and no two seasons, days, or years are exactly the same. Thus, there are cold days in the summer, warm days in the winter, rainy days in the fall, and dry days in the spring. The pattern is familiar but the details vary in a more or less unpredictable way. Here the overall weather pattern is the attractor, created by the unique combination of sunlight, humidity, and barometric pressure in any particular geographic region. But unlike the case of the pendulum, this pattern constantly varies in a way that cannot be predicted in detail. For this reason it is termed a *chaotic attractor*, sometimes called a *strange attractor*, meaning that it subscribes to the mathematics of chaos theory. The term *strange attractor* was given to such attractors by the first mathematicians who discovered them, observing that they were like cyclic attractors that act "strange."

Most highly complex systems, those made up of many elements which themselves are also complex, tend to behave like chaotic attractors. The weather is an excellent example, but others include the metabolic cycles of the human body, the ecologies of rainforests, the international stock market, and neural activity in the human brain. All of these are complex systems that exhibit identifiable big-picture patterns of behavior, but are not predictable in minute to minute or day to day detail. It seems that human consciousness is much the same. It is the product of many complex interacting factors, some of them biological, some situational, and many of them the psychological functions that Tart originally identified, all of which combine to form a chaotic attractor pattern that we call consciousness or experience. For instance, this morning as I write I am still vaguely aware of pleasant feelings still fresh from the concert I experienced last night, in which the wonderful violinist Joshua Bell played Beethoven's *Concerto in D minor*. At the same time my mind is filled with a certain nostalgia for my wife, still in Ohio, as I write in San Francisco. Meanwhile I am absorbed in the thoughts that I write on this page, and reflections on how best to phrase them, all the while aware of the beauty of the fall day. All of these elements, each a process in itself, each reflecting its own mental stream, each represented in a different vector of neurological activity in my brain, come together to form the unique strange attractor that creates my conscious experience in this moment and which will guide that experience through changing conditions throughout the day and throughout my life.

This complex chaotic attractor of experience, of course, is nothing less than William James' "stream of consciousness." And it tends by its very nature, by the mutual fit and simpatico of the processes that comprise it, to flow through ordinary waking consciousness, dream consciousness, drug-created states of consciousness, etc. These states of consciousness tend to rest each in their own *attractor basins*, a term from the sciences of complexity. Each attractor, cyclic or chaotic, can be thought of as captured in such a basin. To help picture this situation, imagine that a state of consciousness is a marble rolling on a tabletop into which various shallow and deep hollows or basins have been carved. If the marble approaches one of these it will roll down inside it. The steeper the slope, the deeper the bottom of the basin, the greater will be its influence over the marble. What is more, the deeper the basin the greater the force necessary to pop the marble out of it and back onto the tabletop where it can then proceed, as it were, on to other basins. Ordinary waking consciousness represents a deep basin, meaning that it is difficult to dislodge a person from it. The same is true for dream sleep. Indeed, it is as hard to wake a person out of the dream state as it is from the deepest stages of non-dream sleep.

Stabilizing states of consciousness and changing from one to another

Charles Tart listed four general types of influences that help stabilize and maintain a state of consciousness. He expressed these in cybernetic terms.[10] The first is *loading stabilization*, which means to load the conscious system with some activity that draws it into a particular state and keeps it there. Ordinary waking consciousness, for instance, is stabilized by productive work. Paint the house, mow the lawn, cook meals, wash dishes, write email letters, pay bills. All these activities and many others nail you down in ordinary waking consciousness for as long as you continue to do them. Certain meditative states, on the other hand, are stabilized by repeating a mantra, observing the flow of breath, chanting with others, or dancing in circles as do Sufi Dervishes.

The second type is *negative feedback stabilization*, in which tendencies to exit the state trigger negative consequences. For instance, in traditional Zazen meditation when the student begins to nod off to sleep the instructor may give him or her a sound crack across the shoulder with a large paddle! This is intended not as punishment, but rather to help the student stay awake during, for example, a predawn sitting session. Likewise, in a traditional nineteenth century school setting a student may receive a whack on the knuckles from a hard stick if caught daydreaming, that is, drifting off into a state of reverie.

Positive feedback, the third type, occurs when one becomes increasing drawn into a state of consciousness because of its positive effects. We might call it the "you can't eat just one" effect! For example, if you are feeling satisfaction in the work you are doing while in normal waking consciousness you are likely to stay right there with it instead, for instance, of taking a nap! Another example is the experience of positive feelings during meditation states, allowing one to be drawn further and further into the meditative experience. Many types of "recreational drugs" have associated positive feelings, so that a small dose leads one to want more. This, of course, can be a serious problem if the drug is addictive.

Limiting stabilization occurs when some absolute boundary is put on the situation. It sounds a bit like negative feedback stabilization, but is not necessarily negative and is more absolute. For instance, when I fly somewhere in a different time zone, especially one that is several hours different than the time I am used to, I have a personal rule not to go to sleep before the local bedtime. This is my way of managing jet lag. But it is easier said than done if you have spent the last 36 hours in airports and on airplanes. How I manage it is to go walking. If it is not dead winter I eat dinner then go walking about the city, or wherever I am, until it is reasonable for me to go to bed. This makes it virtually impossible for me to fall asleep. In fact, I don't even have to fight sleep. And then later I collapse. This is an example of limiting stabilization.

Of course, even with these four types of stabilization to lock-in states of consciousness we do actually shift from one state to another, that is, from one attractor basin to another, several times during each 24-hour period. At a minimum we experience wakefulness, dream sleep, which might involve any of a number of different states, non-dream sleep, and possibly others as well. For those who meditate the latter might include one or more meditative states. They might also include drug-induced states, depending on a person's use of medicinal or recreational drugs. They might include various pathological states, and so on. The question in each instance is how we make the transitions, or in terms of conscious states as attractors, how we escape from one attractor basin and move on to others.

Tart explains such transitions in terms of positive *patterning influences* and negative *disruptive influences*. Patterning influences are just what they sound like; they tend to pattern us into one state of consciousness or another. For instance, when we want to enjoy a good night's sleep we put down the tasks and responsibilities of the day, change into whatever clothes (or absence of clothes) we like to sleep in, wash and brush our teeth—which also serves as a kind of transition ritual—and lie down in a dark room on a soft mattress and, perhaps, turn on some quiet relaxing music. All this helps prepare us for an easy transition into restful sleep. It is also helpful to get in the habit of going to bed at roughly the same time each night, as this puts the body into the proper circadian rhythm. If all this is not enough to induce sleep, a bit of warm milk and a cracker can be helpful.

Patterning forces are used in many cultures to produce profoundly altered states of consciousness. Deep states of meditation, for example, are achieved by practicing certain sitting postures, regulating the breath, and applying such mental exercises as the repetition of a sacred word or phrase. Shamans throughout the world are trained to enter alternative experiential worlds, above and below the ordinary world in which we live. Some use potent chemical agents to assist with this transition, but many do not, relying instead on ritual activities including chants and dances combined with years of training and practice. In many primary cultures a combination of dancing, fatigue, and pain effectively facilitate the arrival of altered states of consciousness. Many examples could also be given in which long periods of dancing without rest, or physical pain combined with fatigue are used to initiate sacred visions or other numinous experiences.[11] The point here is that virtually all experiences of non-ordinary reality are triggered or initiated by some form of patterning stimuli.

Disruptive influences work in the opposite fashion, disrupting our present state of consciousness and hence freeing us of its attractor. This sets us free to move into alternative states of consciousness. Disruptive influences come in a variety of forms, all of which make it difficult to impossible to remain in whatever state we are presently experiencing. For instance, loud noises or other strong physical stimuli tend to wake us from sleep. Chemical stimulants such as caffeine not only tend to pattern us into a condition of arousal, but also disrupt relaxed or sleepy states. This is why we drink coffee or other caffeine-based beverages when we begin to drowse while driving. On the other hand, a modest quantity of alcohol such as a glass of wine or beer helps relieve tense feelings after a stressful day. From such examples it is apparent that disruptive influences are simply the backside of patterning influences. That is, a particular stimulus, drug, or activity is often disruptive to one state of consciousness, say sleep, because it is at the same time facilitating another state.

I will have more to say about states of consciousness below, but since states are virtually never experienced in the absence of structures, let us now turn our attention to an examination of the structures of consciousness.

Structures of consciousness

A *structure of consciousness* refers to the way in which the mind takes hold of an experience and makes it its own. To put this slightly differently, a structure of consciousness is the way the mind *interprets* the moment, modifying the raw stuff of experience according to its own habits and categories. An interesting feature of structures of consciousness, however, is that we cannot perceive them directly. They are, rather, the ways in which we perceive everything else. In a sense we are on the inside looking out at the world and even at ourselves. But since we have nowhere to stand that is truly outside ourselves, we must rely on external cues and reports from others to learn about our own structures.

In his book, *Integral Spirituality*, Wilber uses an example of a poker game to discuss these notions. I will do the same. If we observe a game objectively, say, by sitting near the table but not actually playing—or better yet, watching it on TV where one can see all the cards—it may, in time, be possible to identify the patterns of behaviors that make up the game and even guess the underlying pattern of rules that govern these behaviors. Such an objective analysis is the typical approach of *structuralism* as a discipline or type of inquiry. Jean Piaget's studies of the cognitive growth of children discussed in the previous two chapters are illustrative of such an approach. Now, if we understand the rules of poker well enough to reflect on the game as a whole, that is, if we understand the *idea* of poker, then we are grasping the *pattern* of concepts that make up the game. In all of this, however, we have not yet touched on the *pattern of experience* that actually characterizes the game for the players. To understand that pattern you must sit down at the table and play the game yourself. Needless to say, it is precisely that pattern, the pattern of experience, that holds the game's attraction and brings the players back to the table again and again.

Note that in reality all of these patterns overlay each other as aspects of a single overarching manifold we refer to as the game of poker. If you are actually playing the game, however, it is unlikely that you will be experiencing all of them. In fact, if you are new to the game you may only know the rules well enough to get by with the help of the other players. And only a seasoned player is likely to have a well-developed conceptual understanding of the game as a whole. On the other hand, every player has a complete *experience* of playing the game. How could it be otherwise? These experiences, however, will be different depending on the player's level of mastery and how long he or she has been playing. Thus, more seasoned players will make use of different and more sophisticated strategies than will a novice, who may be relying almost entirely on luck. Such a player may win a hand or two from time to time, but is unlikely to show a consistent pattern of winning. Now let us turn from the game of poker to structures of consciousness.

Piaget was the first researcher to map in detail how patterns of thinking change as we grow and mature, and how these determine our experience of reality. As we have seen, he was mainly interested in children and adolescents. He asked young people carefully worded questions that disclosed their ways of understanding themselves and the world in which they lived. In doing so, he was always seeking to understand the underlying patterns of thought and knowledge.[12] What he discovered was that our sensory experiences, as well as our inner thoughts, feelings, and memories, are refracted though habitual structures of interpretation to such an extent that we literally live in different experiential worlds as we pass through infancy, childhood, adolescence, and so on. Piaget observed that these interpretative structures fall into distinct categories during development, which he identified as sensory-motor behavior, pre-operational thinking, concrete operations thinking, and formal operations thinking,[13] pointing out that everyone goes through these stages in the same order, and that they are evidently universal in one form or anther to the human condition.

Now, if we turn the objective, or structuralist, perspective of our poker game inside out we get to the actual experience of the player: what it is like to be playing poker. Similarly, we might ask what it is like to experience reality through sensory-motor, preoperational, concrete operational, or formal operational thinking and perception. We might then talk about the preoperational level in terms of how it structures the everyday experience of a child, or of an adult who has not matured beyond this to the more advanced stages of mental growth. These patterns of experience are nothing less than *structures of consciousness.*

While Piaget and his colleagues taught us a great deal about the mind and experience of the child, and thus the experiential worlds of children, they did not actually speak in terms of "structures of consciousness." The first person to do this was Piaget's contemporary, Jean Gebser, a European poet and cultural historian who recognized a progression of such structures that seem to have unfolded, step by step, across the long course of human history. Other scholars later recognized his historical sequence to be strikingly similar to the series of structures that Piaget was discovering at more or less the same time in children.[14] While Piaget identified his structures by the terms we are now familiar with such as "pre-operational," "concrete operations," and so on—each identifying some basic aspect of the mind of the child—Gebser's terms were descriptive of the *worldview* implicit in each structure of consciousness: *archaic, magic, mythic, mental,* and *integral.* I will have more to say about these soon, but briefly the structures line up as shown in Table 6.1.

| JEAN PIAGET | JEAN GEBSER |
DEVELOPMENTAL STRUCTURES	HISTORICAL WORLDVIEWS
Formal Operational	Mental
Concrete Operational	Mythic
Preoperational	Magic
Sensory-Motor	Archaic

Table 6.1. Piaget and Gebser Structures

Gebser's "integral structure," of which we will have more to say later, is not included in Table 6.1 because it has no counterpart in Piaget's system. We have reviewed some of the experiential aspects of each of Piaget's developmental structures in Chapters 4 and 5. Let us now take a few moments to examine the corresponding structures of consciousness in terms of Gebser's worldviews.

Structures of consciousness as worldviews

Each of these worldviews, or structures of consciousness as Gebser called them, like each of Piaget's developmental stages, identifies an entire experiential landscape. Put more simply, each is a complete way of understanding and relating to the world. At bottom they represent modes of perceiving and understanding reality. We saw this in Piaget's stages and it is even more apparent in Gebser's worldviews. The latter also identifies historical epochs in which each structure rose to the status of a dominant adult worldview. This does not mean that during each of these epochs every adult experienced the same worldview. In fact, these epochs overlapped considerably. And within each of them there were differences between people, as indeed there are today. For instance, the dominant structure during the twentieth century has been the mental worldview, at least throughout much of the world. This is equivalent in Piaget's terms to formal operations thinking. This does not mean, however, that everyone was functioning at this level, even among adults. In fact, large numbers of people were and still are living in the mythic and even the magic worldviews. It is just a question of which structures tend to dominate social decisions and values at any point in history. Basically, it is a matter of how people tend to answer questions such as these:

> Where did the world come from, and what is it made of?
>
> What is the ultimate fate of the world and of humanity?
>
> Who am I?
>
> Where did I come from?
>
> What is my role here?
>
> What will happen to me after death?

Worldviews through time:
the magic structure of consciousness

Gebser believed, with considerable justification, that entire Paleolithic cultures operated in the magic mode of consciousness. In such a world natural events like lightning, rainbows, or earthquakes, might portend future events, good hunting, or the death of someone in the tribe. He believed that in magical cultures magical phenomena such as telepathy and synchronicities may well have been common occurrences. The spiritual life of such communities most likely centered on local shamans who, like shamans in many parts of the world today, acted as both spiritual guides and healers, looking after the physical as well as the spiritual wellbeing of the people. Shamans often enter into altered states of consciousness to travel in the upper or lower worlds, and may serve as psychopomps, leading recently deceased souls to their destinations in the afterlife. Shamans typically receive help in their many tasks from power animals, spirits that make it possible for them to successfully achieve their goals. Interestingly, Gebser considered modern "witchcraft," which involves the manipulation of nature rather than working in simpatico with it, to be a lesser and degenerate form of the original use of magic.

In the world of magical consciousness time and space have not solidified into the Newtonian worldview that characterizes modern-day mental consciousness. Time is cyclic, based on the succession of the days, the moon, and the seasons. "This time next year" literally means *this very same time* next year, not next year at this time. Time and space are less definite and more permeable as well. This is the basis of magic: I do something here and now, and it has an effect, or more correctly speaking it is also taking place, somewhere else or at another time. Gebser tells a story of an African pygmy getting ready to go out hunting for a giraffe.[15] Before leaving the village he drew an image of a giraffe in the sand and shot it through the neck with an arrow. Later in the day he returned to the village with a small giraffe displaying an arrow in the same location in its neck. Now, the point about the pre-hunting morning ritual is not that he was practicing or "warming up" for the hunt. He was actually slaying the giraffe magically before going out to finish the job on the living animal. In a similar vein, there are examples of drawings as well as clay sculptures of animals found in the Paleolithic caves of southern Europe that appear to have been struck repeatedly by sharp objects, very likely in magical rituals that accompanied actual hunting expeditions.

Gebser pointed out that the magic structure of consciousness is still very much with us in many positive as well as negative ways. For instance the sense of oneness we feel with those we love is a positive expression of magical consciousness. Magical consciousness is also connected with music, and especially the ability of music to transport us away from the here and now to "the land behind the music," as writer Thomas Mann expressed it. On the other hand it is the call of the magical consciousness that can draw us away from our modern personal consciousness and the self-awareness that it makes possible, into mass movements in which individual consciousness is dissolved into a more or less mindless group. This happened in Germany during the rise of the Third Reich. All you have to do to get a powerful whiff of the dark side of this kind of thing is listen to some of the political rallies in which Hitler would charge up thousands of followers for his so-called Aryan cause. The overall sense of the crowd crying out is like some huge dark animal roaring deep in the earth. It would be good for us to take this history as a cautionary lesson so that we in the U.S. do not follow this path in the face of contemporary world threats.

Magic for both good and evil is usually initiated by rituals, and Freud was perhaps the first to recognize that many neurotic defense mechanisms operate in this fashion as well. Compulsive behavior, for example, falls into this category, in which certain actions such as hand-washing are carried out obsessively and ritually in an effort to control anxiety or guilt. The defense mechanisms of repression and projection are other examples.

Repression is nothing less than an effort to make some impulse, thought, feeling, or perception go away by convincing oneself that it doesn't exist. This is plain and simple magic, though only marginally effective, as every psychologist knows. Projection falls into the same category: believing the source of one's own feelings are coming from someone else. I may believe that my supervisor at work, for example, dislikes me, when in fact I am only covering my own feelings of insecurity or inadequacy, perhaps with origins that go all the way back to my childhood and the way my own mother treated me. These and many other examples of confused and neurotic behavior have their roots in magical thinking of the kind first seen in young children during the preoperational period of development.

The mythic structure of consciousness

It is difficult to give even a rough dating to when these worldviews came into ascendance and when they receded again to a less prominent position. Nevertheless, it is helpful to have some idea of what historical periods we are talking about. For the magical worldview, a survey of the archeological evidence seems clearly to place the world of Paleolithic humankind, that is the Old Stone Age, as a time of ascendance for magical experience, at least in Europe if not elsewhere as well. This was a world of small hunting and gathering communities in which magic and spirituality were essentially the same thing, and guidance concerning both was given by the tribal shaman. At this writing it is virtually impossible to put a beginning date on this period, extending back as it does, perhaps 100,000 or even 200,000 or more years.

Approaching the agricultural revolution that defined the beginning of the Neolithic period, or New Stone Age, which began very roughly around 12,000 years ago, we see a rise in the mythic imagination and with it the mythic worldview. In this structure of consciousness spirituality no longer centers around local spirit animals, but rather we see the emergence of grand mythic themes comparable to those found in modern-day religions. These involved great gods and goddesses that exercise dominion over all the heavens and the earth. The earliest and most prominent was apparently the Earth Mother, or Earth Goddess, represented in the many small figurines found throughout Europe and much of Asia, such as the "Venus of Willendorf" (Figure 6.1). These were typically only a few inches tall, and represented women with large full breasts and round abdomens, sometimes visibly pregnant. After much debate the general conclusion about them is that they represent the fertility and life-giving aspect of the earth in the form of the Mother Goddess.

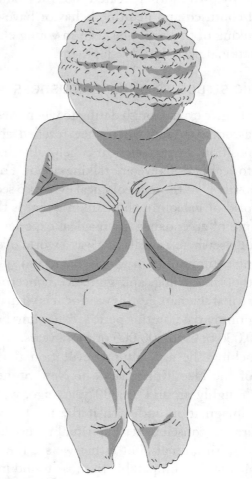

Figure 6.1: Venus of Willendorf

The prominent mythologist, Joseph Campbell, referred to the spirituality surrounding these figures as a full-blown religion of the naked Goddess. This goddess was also recognized in various ancient traditions as the Consort of the Moon-bull, the Lady of the Wild Things, and the Protector of the Hearth.[16] The goddess appears to have been associated with the feminine in general, the night and the mystery of the night and darkness, the moon in its phases, with snakes and healing, and with a heavenly bull. The phases of the moon reflect the monthly cycle of women, and the crescent moon is strongly reminiscent of the bull horns of the goddess' heavenly consort. Snakes were associated symbolically and perhaps literally with healing. Indeed, the modern physician's staff, the *caduceus*, still presents two snakes entwined about a staff with wings at the top.

With the rise of the ancient civilizations of the Middle East, the supremacy of the goddess and all she stood for gave way to the rise of a generation of male-dominated sky gods. We are familiar with these from the "ancient" mythologies of Greece, Egypt, and the Fertile Crescent. The ascent of the Mesopotamian god, Marduk, was associated with a great battle in which he literally dismembered Tiamat, the ruling goddess who represented the old lineage of the Earth Mother.[17] Other sky gods such as Horus, in Egypt, came into power in less overtly violent ways, but in each case the shift in power went to warrior-like god figures such as Marduk, Horus, and Zeus, each associated with the sky, the sun, the brilliance of day, and each symbolized by a great predator bird such as the eagle for Zeus and the hawk for Horus. We might also recall that Moses approached Jehovah, in Hebraic tradition, only by ascending high onto a mountain.

Much has been written about the powerful male gods, the mythic religions they represented, and how the deep shift from the nurturing feminine to the dominating masculine has affected the world ever since, especially Western civilization where this transition was most spectacular.[18] It would take us far afield to explore this topic in detail, but one of the important aspects of this shift in terms of the history of consciousness was an accompanying transition away from a feminine emphasis on community towards a masculine emphasis on action and agency. The earliest expressions of the latter seem to have been in the form of rather violent egotism, as evidenced by the conquests of the warrior kings of ancient Greece and Mesopotamia. Homer's *Iliad*, for instance, is a story of conflict between the great warriors of Greece and Troy. If the events described in the *Iliad* actually took place they probably occurred somewhere around 1200 B.C.E., while the epic poem itself was most likely created much later, perhaps around the eighth century B.C.E. The events described in the Sumerian tale of Gilgamesh were older, perhaps dating back to around 2600 B.C.E., while the earliest written forms of the story may be as old as 2000 to 2100 B.C.E. In this story the hero-king Gilgamesh battles Ishtar, the queen of heaven, in yet another example of the rise of masculine dominance over the feminine principle. Like Odysseus in the *Iliad* and in its sequel, the *Odyssey*, Gilgamesh is an intelligent man, even leaning toward existential speculation in his search for the soul of his deceased friend, Enkidu, and the meaning of life itself.

The mythic worldview sees reality in terms of sweeping epics involving gods and goddesses, and grand vistas of creation and the fate of the world. The Abrahamic religions, for instance, all share a version of the same root story of the creation of the world by a single god and the early hardships and adventures of God's chosen people, the Hebrews. Later, these religions split into the Christian, Islamic, and the Jewish faiths. Each has its own mythic story of the essential meaning of life and humankind's place and purpose in the world. What is important to understand here, as Gebser would point out, is not whether these stories are historically or scientifically factual, but how they lend a sense of spirituality and purpose to the lives of those who invest in them. The establishment of scientific truth, like the fixing of historical accuracy, is a passion of the mental structure of consciousness, which we will turn to shortly, and not a concern of the mythic mind. Indeed, the whole effort to "prove" the historical accuracy of the life of Christ and other

Biblical narratives only arose in biblical scholarship during the twentieth century.

For those who lived in mythic times, history was not linear, as it is in mental time, and questions of scientific validation have little meaning. Time, in fact, is experienced as what Gebser termed "temporicity." For instance, one might speak of the events that occurred "in the days of" King Arthur and the Knights of the Round Table. Fairy tales take place in a world of mythic time, as announced in the opening phrase, "long ago and far away." We can even experience recent historical times in the mythic way, as is done in nostalgic remembrances of John F. Kennedy's America, romantically named "Camelot." Or, we can think of times in our own lives in this mythic fashion, such as a happy summer in childhood; recalling it, for instance, as "the Summer of '73" when I fell in love for the first time.

The mental structure of consciousness

In Western civilization the mental structure of consciousness came into its own when people began to answer basic questions about the nature of the world though logic and reason. It first appeared in the West in the pre-Socratic philosophers such as Thales (624-546 B.C.E.), Anaximander (610-546 B.C.E.) and Anaximenes of Miletus (585-525 B.C.E.), who took hold of older mythic ideas and began to reason objectively with them, gradually leading to new and more logically systematic theories of the material world. This does not mean that people could not, or did not, use reason to solve problems during earlier times. It just means that such reason was not the final arbitrator of truth. Needless to say, we are talking about the important leading edge of the mental structure of consciousness because there are many people who even today do not make judgments based on logic and reason. Such folks may rely on mythic or even magical ideas to dictate many of their choices. This is an observation that we also made in Chapter 5 in terms of cognitive development.

The mental structure tended to dominate the ancient Greek and Roman worlds, as evidenced in politics, especially through the ideal of a citizen's rights and the duties of participation in government. This does not mean that the average citizen of antiquity did not subscribe to any of the variety of mythic religions that competed in the ancient Mediterranean world until late in into antiquity when Christianity finally came to dominate all others.

Strangely, it seems that with the fall of Rome the mental structure was largely lost in the West during the Middle Ages, from roughly 500–1500 A.D., though it continued to survive in Persia and the Eastern Roman Empire. A mythic Christian worldview dominated virtually all thought during this long period of darkness, and Western civilization waited patiently though the long slow changes that prepared it for the coming Renaissance. The latter appeared in the great cities of Italy during the fourteenth and fifteenth centuries, shortly after the Black Plague had dramatically diminished the population of Europe, shifting wealth into the hands of fewer people and dramatically reducing the availability of skilled laborers and craftsman, and stimulating the rise of a new middle class.

Here it is worth noting that much of this discussion directs itself to the history of Western civilization. There is good reason to suspect that transformations not unlike those seen in the West occurred or are occurring in other civilizations as well, though perhaps not at the same times. There are limits to what can be treated in this relatively small book, though it is hoped that future scholarship will encompass ever wider circles of what it means to be human.

Perspectival consciousness

The appearance of the Renaissance in Italy, and its upward spread though Europe, brought with it a vigorous resurgence of the mental structure of consciousness which soon found itself battling openly with mythic ideas still held strongly by the Roman Catholic Church. The story of its victory in the creation of the Age of Enlightenment, and its heroes such as Galileo Galilei, Johannes Kepler, Tycho Brahe, René Descartes, Isaac Newton, and others, is widely celebrated. Here, however, our interest is in the appearance during the Renaissance of a dramatically new form of mental structure which Gebser termed *perspectival consciousness*. First perfected in art and architecture as *perspective*, by Filippo Brunelleschi and Leonardo da Vinci, this shift represented a subtle but powerful new way of experiencing the world.

The artists of the Renaissance became interested in depicting the physical world realistically. In doing so they became fascinated with new discoveries in drawing, painting, and architecture that allow the artist or architect to endow a work of art with a palpable sense of depth and proportion. It is as if painters had discovered a way to punch through the canvas, making it into a virtual window through which the observer views a natural landscape, or the exact proportions of the interior of a room or cathedral.

Figure 6.2a: Drawing by Brunelleschi depicting depth perspective.

Figure 6.2b: Church of San Lorenzo, designed by Brunelleschi in Florence.

The discovery of the laws of perspective represented a major transition in the history of art. But it also created a dramatic shift in how people began to experience the world itself. This is because it *de facto* places the observer in a specific location with respect to the canvas, or work of architecture. If you look at a medieval painting you will find that you seem to be in a kind of indefinite space before it, with no specific point of view. In a perspectival work, however, you find yourself observing the subject of the work of art from a specific position in relation to it. In some instances this fixing of the location of the observer is so powerful that the eyes of the subject in the painting seem to follow you about the room as you move back and forth in front of the painting. My point is that perspective not only organized space into depth and proportion, but it also locks the observer down to a particular point from which his or her observation takes place. Physicist and cultural historian David Peat likes to say that it is as if the observer's head is clamped into a device that allows only one's eyes to rotate this way and that, but does not permit movement of the head.

Now, all of this is fine and good in terms of art history, but what does it have to do with the transformation of consciousness? Well, the big change occurred as people began to carry this way of experiencing the world away from art itself and into their daily lives. To be more specific, it meant that each person began to see the world quite literally from his or her own point of view. This amounted to a kind of position-bound ego that seems to be located in the head somewhere between or just above the location of the eyes. For instance, if you ask most people to point to where their consciousness seems to be located they will point to their heads. Now, this was not always the case. The ancient Greeks would have pointed to their hearts, and there are many instances in ancient writings of someone asking of someone else, "Who put that idea into your heart?" Gebser observed that the heart is intimately associated with the mythic mode of experience, whereas the head, and even the sense of a particular point in the head somewhere behind the eyes, is associated with the location of perspectival mental consciousness.

We can see from all this that perspectival consciousness brought with it a lot of extra baggage, not the least of which was a sense of specific location, and along with that a feeling of isolation and detachment from the rest of the world which seems to expand out before us. Gebser pointed out that during the Renaissance the world was indeed expanding in many directions. Ancient maps, some preserved from antiquity in Persia and Greece, were rediscovered and brought to Italy, the center of the Renaissance and the new way of thinking. The size of the world was literally growing by leaps and bounds. Explorers traveled from Italy, Spain, and Portugal to explore a global topography that was becoming enormous in scope, while astronomers such as Galileo and Kepler were discovering a new universe in which the Earth was only a small part. This process of expansion has continued right up to the present day. Pick up any popular book or magazine on science and you will find descriptions of black holes, galactic clusters, and even multiple universes filled with billions upon billions of stars. All this threatens to leave the perspectival mind swimming in vastness and overwhelmed with its own smallness and isolation.

But it gets worse. The plain fact is that the cultural, moral, and political realities of the twenty-first century are complex beyond the ability of the mental perspectival mind to cope with. Indeed, it exhibits a tendency to reduce whatever it sees to the smallest common denominator and then to wrangle with it. This propensity, which Gebser termed *ratio* (literally "division"), leads to constant disputes over small issues. In time it gives birth not only to mean-spirited academic and philosophical squabbles, but more importantly to political and religious disputes and ultimately to physical aggression and wars.

To thrive in the world today means to peacefully and successfully cope with the diverse and intricate social realities in which we all live. This requires a suppleness of mind and spirit that permits us not only to tolerate, but to appreciate and even enjoy the multiplicity of cultural, religious, and moral lifestyles that we see each day in the news, and which many of us encounter whenever we step out the front door and onto the street. Clearly the mental structure, even in its perspectival form, is in over its head.

The integral structure of consciousness

Gebser believed that a major new structure of consciousness was coming into existence around the end of the nineteenth century and the beginning of the twentieth century. He called it the integral structure of consciousness, and he found evidence for this in many quarters, including music, poetry, jurisprudence, science, mathematics, and art. This new form of experience was highly flexible compared to the perspectival mental structure, affording a variety of perspectives at once. Picasso's paintings of models, and especially his famous 1937 rendering of the bombing of Guernica, are examples of this kind of nimbleness of view. So is the 1925 mathematical modeling of time and space in Heisenberg's matrix mathematics which formed the basis of physics' new quantum mechanics.

Integral consciousness also escapes linear time as conceptualized by Newtonian perspectival consciousness. Rather than a scalar quantity that can be measured and represented, for example in a Cartesian coordinate system along beside length and depth, time becomes a poetic-like quality. Algis Mickunas, co-translator of Gebser's major work, *The Ever-Present Origin*, gives the example of snow falling during the night. A mental perspectival understanding of the snow would specify when it fell according to clock time. "It snowed between three and five o'clock this morning." But an integral experience of the snow might emphasize that it is, "The night's snow; the gift of the night," or some other poetic representation emphasizing the quality of the experience of the night and the snow, rather than abstracting an event outside of experience that presumably occurred during a particular episode of clock time. This sense of qualitative, or poetic time, is experienced in the works of certain poets such as Rainer Maria Rilke, whom Gebser knew personally, and the American poet Wallace Stevens.

Stevens' wonderful poem, *Thirteen Ways of Looking at a Blackbird*, has a dark and magical quality while simultaneously being luminous. Gebser referred to this luminous quality as "diaphany," a translucent spiritual light that shines through the world of integral experience. Paradoxically, this magical quality in Stevens' poem is consistent with Gebser's notion of integral experience as bringing together all the structures of consciousness into a single living fabric. Indeed, integral consciousness, from Gebser's point of view, is essentially characterized by this integration of all the structures in a single lived experience.

I will have more to say about the integral structure of consciousness. At this point I only note that at the time Gebser was developing these ideas he had not been exposed to the notion that there may be a hierarchy of experiential structures that extend well beyond the mental and the ordinary. On reflection, I suspect that many of the qualities that he attributed to a single integral structure of consciousness are actually features of a number of these higher and more refined structures. It is, perhaps, as if

Gebser were looking through these higher structures vertically, and thus seeing their qualities telescoped into a single view. Now let us proceed to the next chapter where we will explore some of these higher structures as they are understood today.

7. The Hierarchy of Minds

> In the third stage, the super-logical, the mind seeks to return to immediacy, to solve the dualism and oppositions inherent in the practical life of thought and action. One or another of the great ideals arises and becomes the place of retreat; and the universal categories of thought, the absolute forms of value, and the various panaceas of feeling erect their claims to final authority. [And so in the grand scheme] the leading motives of development [are seen passing] from perception and memory, through the various phases of the reasoning processes, and finding their consummation in the highest and most subtle of the super-logical, rational, and mystic states of mind.
>
> —*James Mark Baldwin, 1930* [1]

During the early decades of the twentieth century the American psychologist James Mark Baldwin came to view development in the individual, and thus the maturing of conscious experience, as spanning three major epochs. The first he referred to as *pre-logical*, meaning the pre-logical experience of the child; the second he termed *logical*, referring to the ordinary adult stage in which thought is governed by reasoning; and a third he called *super-logical*, indicating a shift to a more profound, intuitive, and universal way of understanding the world. We are already familiar with the first of these as a combination of Piaget's preoperational and concrete operational stages, and the second as Piaget's formal operations thinking. The third, however, points to higher and less common realms of thought. We explore these territories in the pages that follow.

Baldwin's three-part division is still employed by theorists today, including Ken Wilber and me; we often substitute the descriptive terms, *preconventional*, *conventional*, and *postconventional*, in recognition of the fact that ordinary adult development is commonly referred to as "conventional." The key point is that Baldwin was directing us to a dimension of growth that stretched beyond ordinary logic and reasoning towards a more profound and immediate grasp of truth. Baldwin, however, was not the only theorist during the early decades of the twentieth century to recognize the importance of the advanced stages of mind. Sri Aurobindo, the Indian sage and yogi, was also mapping such stages of transformation. He described a whole series of developmental levels that carry the growth of the human spirit into extraordinary realms of possibility.

Following the same line of thought as Baldwin and Sri Aurobindo, Wilber (2000b) more recently surveyed a broad range of theoretical writings on stages of mental and spiritual development both in modern psychology and from traditional wisdom sources. His summary of the advanced stages is shown in Table 7.1.

6	Supermind	Associated with satchitananda or nondual experience
5	Overmind	Traditional causal realm experience
4	Intuitive Mind	Traditional subtle or "higher subtle" experience
3	Illumined Mind	Traditional "psychic" or "lower subtle" experience
◄ Transition		from Conventional to Postconventional Mind ►
2	Integralism	Global holism; Aurobindo's Higher Mind; late vision logic
1	Pluralism	Understanding context, relativistic; early vision-logic

Table 7.1. Stages beyond formal operations.[2]

Entries 1 and 2 in Table 7.1, *pluralism* and *integralism*, represent the upper reaches of conventional thinking. Of them Wilber observes, "They are the highest reaches of the mental realms, to be sure, but beyond them lie supramental and properly transrational developments."[3]

In *pluralism* one becomes increasingly aware of the importance of context in understanding just about everything. Topics as diverse as politics, economics, biology, and human relationships all require an understanding of surrounding circumstances. Those who are unable to do this, through a lack of reflection, poor education, or plain old laziness, cling to simplistic and even destructive solutions to the complex and difficult problems that life presents us. During the 1950s and 1960s William Perry of Harvard University conducted an in-depth investigation of the intellectual development of a group of Harvard and Radcliffe students.[4] His results showed that as these remarkably bright young people moved through college they gradually changed their way of thinking from initially seeking "correct" answers from authoritative professors to the realization that correct answers are context-bound. The best interpretation of *Hamlet* in today's world was not the best interpretation, say, 100 years ago. Even scientific "truths" change through time when the surrounding assumptions of the scientific community change, as Thomas Kuhn illustrated so clearly in his classic book, *The Structure of Scientific Revolutions*.[5]

In the language of psychological growth, Harvard's Robert Kegan refers to pluralism as "stage 4" or *self-authorship*, because an increasing awareness of multiple frames of reference at this stage is also associated with a growing sense of choice and responsibility.[6] In short, young people realize that it is up to them to find their own way in a complex world. Different families, different religions, and different ethnicities, to name but a few, each have their own traditions, values, expectations, and beliefs. An increasing awareness of these disparities leads to a dawning realization of the extent to which all this is context-bound and hence ultimately arbitrary, thus inviting and even requiring us to make our own choices. This is the beginning of an existential awareness.

Integralism, or *vision-logic*, is the highest level of conventional mind. From its vantage point whole systems of thought are seen in relationship to each other. This is Kegan's "stage 5," which he considers to be the minimal level of intellectual mastery required for effectively navigating the complexities of the postmodern world. It is this level of mind that understands complex systems, including the importance of intricate feedback networks and ideas of multiple causation. Sri Aurobindo referred to this form of intelligence as "higher mind," associating it with the "mental" sheath, or *kosha*, of Vedanta philosophy.[7] This level of mind is experienced by many creative people and is often linked to significant moments of originality which flow down, as it were, from higher aspects of the mind or from an unconscious creative process. For instance, the great French mathematician Henri Poincaré described this flow of creative ideas in the mind of the mathematician as follows:

> Never in the field of [the mathematician's] consciousness do ideas appear that are not really useful, except some that he rejects but which have to some extent the characteristics of useful combinations. All goes on as if the inventor were an examiner of second degree who would only have to question the candidates who had passed a previous examination.[8]

Beginning with the *illumined mind*, the third entry in the above table, Wilber adopts many of the terms originally used by Sri Aurobindo. At this point personal growth seems to take a right turn and starts moving in the direction of wisdom and spirituality rather than toward ever-increasing cognitive skills and intelligence. Let me explain.

Higher mind: Right turn to the spirit

The right turn in personal growth points the individual in the direction of a more immediate and direct perception of reality, a more profound intuitive faculty, an emerging sense of the subtle dimensions of reality, and a palpable selflessness and compassion for others. This progression has been mapped in detail by many wisdom traditions and is also becoming apparent in modern psychological research.[9]

The illumined mind or lower subtle realm

The *illumined mind* is a phrase that was used by Sri Aurobindo to identify the first of several stages of growth best characterized not only as postconventional but also as spiritual. This stage seems to have an intimate connection with the subtle realm, which in Western esoteric traditions has often been referred to as the *psychic* (or *astral*) realm or "plane." Here we will address it simply as a particular style of thought and level of awareness. Wilber (2000) commonly refers to it as the *lower subtle*.

The illumined mind lies at the beginning of the subtle realms of experience (Table 7.1) and is sometimes associated with the "soul"[10] because it is uniquely individual, on the one hand, and striving toward its luminous origins on the other. This idea is symbolized by the image of the water lily with its roots deep in the earthly mud at the bottom of the river, while stretching upward into the air as it reaches toward the sun.

Resting at the juncture between the material world below and subtle realms above, the illumined mind is associated with various healing practices in which lower subtle or psychic energies, such as *prana* and *chi*, are manipulated to aid a person's health. Because it lies at the border between the material world and the subtle realms, Wilber suggests that the illumined mind is linked with *nature mysticism*: peak experiences triggered by the beauty and power of the world of nature. Anyone who has known the beauty of a quiet forest glade on a summer afternoon, listened to the call of birds over a pristine lake or the sea in the early morning, or seen the majesty of the aurora borealis, is no stranger to such experiences.

The intuitive mind or higher subtle realm

At this level the mind opens to a kind of divine luminosity often associated with *deity mysticism*. Wilber suggests that this is why saints are often depicted with halos of light around their heads. He cites the following passage from Dante's *Divine Comedy* as an illustration of this experience:[11]

Fixing my gaze upon the Eternal Light

I saw within its depths,

Bound up with love together in one volume,

The scattered leaves of all the universe.

Within the luminous profound subsistence

Of that Exalted Light saw I three circles

Of three colors yet of one dimension

And by the second seemed the first reflected

As rainbow is by rainbow, and the third

Seemed fire that equally from both is breathed.[12]

What an incredibly beautiful image! In it we see the mystic theme first to appear at the subtle level of the scattered leaves of all the universe bound up together in one volume. The vision is reminiscent of William Blake's words:

To see a world in a grain of sand

and a heaven in a wild flower,

hold infinity in the palm of your hand

and eternity in an hour.[13]

Both call on a kind of holographic vision of a kosmos in which every facet is reflected throughout the whole, and the whole is mirrored in every part.

Sri Aurobindo noted that when it comes to problem solving, the intuitive mind does not proceed by labored steps of logic but moves forward in strides or leaps, "like a man who springs from one sure spot to another point of sure footing."[14] Certain highly creative persons seem to work from this level of mind. Two well-known examples were Thomas Edison and George Washington Carver. Both were geniuses for whom visions of inventions and discoveries would appear to them full-blown. Edison, who was said to be an atheist, reported that his ideas sprang from the "infinite forces of the universe." Carver, however, went on morning walks in the forest and talked with God. The latter told him what to do when he returned to the laboratory, where Carver would simply follow these directions.[15] Interestingly, he also seemed to be well aware of the next level of experience, the overmind.

The overmind or causal realm

The experience of the overmind represents the deepest known mystical awareness short of full-blown nondual consciousness, if indeed the latter can be called "mystical." From Sri Aurobindo's point of view this mind is the least influenced by the material nature, representing an almost purely divine experience. Speaking from his own experience Wilber describes it in this way:

> Nature retreats before its God, Light finds it own Abode. That's all I keep thinking as I enter into this extraordinary vastness. I am going in and up, in and up, in and up, and I have ceased to have any bodily feelings at all. In fact, I don't even know where my body is, or if I even have one. I know only shimmering sheaths of luminous bliss, each giving way to the next, each softer and yet stronger, brighter and yet fainter, more intense yet harder to see.[16]

The overmind and its association with the causal realm of Vedanta, however, is not without content, or at least so it would seem. Sri Aurobindo writes that "the beings native to the overmind are Gods," and "while [one is] in the overmind…they appear as independent beings."[17] This reflection suggests the presence of powerful and perhaps universal archetypes associated with the experience of the causal realm. For example, historian and mythologist William Irwin Thompson writes of *hieroglyphic thought* that reflects universal patterns of beauty and truth. Examples are found in the music of J.S. Bach, the architecture of Chartres Cathedral, and the celestial harmonics of Pythagoras. Thompson observes that, "The archetypes of melody, figure, equation, and mythic image are like seed crystals from the causal plane; as they are dropped into time, they take time to exfoliate all their compressed possibilities."[18]

Supermind or nondual awareness

There seems to be some variation in the descriptions of this level of experience depending on which source one reads, though it is not clear whether these reflect fundamental differences. Sri Aurobindo referred to the supermind (which he often termed the *supramental*) as a complete shift in the ground of experience away from the brain and the material world to a foundation in the divine. In his view, and that of his partner in yoga The Mother, the true evolutionary work is to stream this pure divine influence down into the ordinary mental and physical levels of being, transforming oneself at each level all the way down to the atoms of the body.[19]

On the other hand, many wisdom traditions emphasize this final stage of spiritual realization as beyond any particular kind of experience, but simply the ground of experience itself.[20] It is the platform, we might say, on which all experience presents itself. Few writers have described this better than Wilber himself:

> In the previous level, you are so absorbed in the unmanifest dimensions that you might not even notice the manifest world. You are discovering Emptiness, and so you ignore Form. But at the ultimate or nondual level, you integrate the two. You see that Emptiness appears or manifests itself as Form, and that Form has as its essence Emptiness. ... All manifestation arises, moment by moment, as a play of Emptiness. If the causal was like a radiant moonlit night, this is like a radiant autumn day.[21]

And,

> This nondual "state" is not itself another experience. It is simply the opening or clearing in which all experiences arise and fall. It is the bright autumn sky through which the clouds come and go—it is not itself another cloud, another experience, another object, another manifestation. This realization is actually of the utter fruitlessness of experience, the utter futility of trying to experience release or liberation.

> All experiences lose their taste entirely—these passing clouds.
> …But you are not apart from the reflections, standing back
> and watching. You *are* everything that is arising moment to
> moment. You can swallow the whole cosmos in one gulp, it
> is so small, and you can taste the entire sky without moving
> an inch.[22]

I will have more to say about nondual awareness when we
examine the Wilber-Combs Lattice.

What research tells us of advanced stages of mental growth

Accounts such as those quoted above are powerful and moving,
and they seem to confirm the maps of experience written centuries
ago by spiritual practitioners from many traditions. Nevertheless,
the modern reader would like to be able to confirm these maps
by means of current research and scholarship. After all, as rich as
such descriptions can be, they tend to represent phenomenological
descriptions and anecdotal experiences of single individuals, and
often reflect the views and beliefs of particular traditions. If
postmodern scholarship teaches us anything it is that virtually all
experiences and beliefs are tempered by the ever-present realities
of culture, history, and language.

Though surprisingly few systematic investigations have
focused on the highest stages of human development, several
recent studies have been reported and more are on the way. These
tend to examine the maturation of the ego and sense of self
beyond the ordinary conventional level. A number of prominent
psychologists have looked at growth above conventional levels,
but few have carried this project to the highest levels.[23] One
good reason for this is that persons who function at such high
psychological levels are not easy to find and study.

Perhaps the most well-known researcher to push the
investigation of stages of psychological growth to extraordinary
heights is Susanne Cook-Greuter,[24] who used Jane Loevinger's
well-researched sentence-completion technique[25] to measure

ego development. She reviewed the self-description protocols for literally thousands of people at many stages of growth. Her dissertation, done under the supervision of Robert Kegan, uncovers three stages of personal growth at the very top of the developmental scale. She termed these the *autonomous stage*, the *construct-aware* (or ego-aware) stage, and the *unitive* stage.

The autonomous stage, or something very much like it, had already been described by several forward-thinking theorists. For example, it is similar to Jenny Wade's[26] "authentic stage," in which individuals are well-grounded and comfortable with themselves, confident in the internal guidance of reason and intuition, enjoy a sense of self-actualization, and are able to resolve most psychological challenges and stresses through their own inner resources. Many readers of this book are in the autonomous stage.

The next stage, that of construct awareness, brings a growing realization of the extent to which one's sense of reality and, indeed, one's very identity are actually the products of complex historical and situational factors that make each of us what we are. Here there is less confidence in an absolute "authentic" sense of self, and a growing and objective sense of one's own thoughts and emotions. With the latter comes an expanding understanding of the limitations inherent in our own deeply entrenched patterns of thought and behavior. All this is experienced within the context of a growing sense of the amazing complexity of ordinary life. Hence the construct aware person may wish to be free of the restrictions of his or her identity, realizing that this identity is ultimately a superficial construct.

The highest level of development that Cook-Greuter was able to identify is the unity stage. A person at this stage has actually achieved the construct aware person's goal of breaking free from deeply-engrained patterns of thought and behavior to live in a kind of moment-to-moment flow of experience. There emerges an "effortlessness, non-control, non-attachment, and radical openness."[27] These rare individuals seem to have achieved a more or less continuous non-judgmental witnessing consciousness, aware of their own thoughts, feelings, and behaviors, and experiencing them as if in a play on the stage of life. Cook-Greuter notes that individuals at this stage seem to live a kind of unbroken peak experience which, unlike the temporary peak experiences of the lower stages of growth, does not seem at all strange or out-of-this-world.

This creative and fluid sense of reality as an undifferentiated phenomenal flow is a radical departure from reliance on the machinations of reason and feeling that structure reality in earlier stages.[28] Along with this there is a sense of oneness or unity that we noted above in the causal and nondual levels of experience. Cook-Greuter quotes from the psychiatrist and sometime mystic R.D. Laing:

> All in all
> Each man in all men
> All men in each man
>
> All being in each being
> Each being in all being
> All in each
> Each in all
>
> All distinctions are mind, by mind,
> in mind, of mind
> No distinctions no mind to
> distinguish [29]

One of the most compelling questions one can ask is how people achieve such high levels of growth. Is it a gift that some are simply born with? Must it be earned as the fruit of a life of rich experiences? Can it be intentionally achieved through effort? Two important studies have recently been reported that give some insight into these questions. One was conducted by Paul Marko[30] and the other by Angela Pfaffenberger.[31] Both researchers interviewed people who had demonstrated high levels of ego development on the same Loevinger scale that Cook-Greuter used in her study. Marko focused his interviews on "facilitative agents," critical experiences that seemed to catalyze psychological growth. As it turns out, these range from insights gained in psychotherapy and elsewhere, to realizations experienced during altered states of consciousness. One participant, for example, reported awakening to a larger reality while on acid at a Grateful Dead concert. Pfaffenberger, on the other hand, did not look for critical experiences in her study. She interviewed her participants informally as well as asking them to write narratives about their own growth and development.

Taking the discoveries from both of these investigators together a rough picture begins to emerge of the "typical" history of a highly evolved person. Perhaps not surprisingly, he or she has experienced a long history during which psychological and spiritual growth have been actively cultivated. Most likely he or she has pursued this interest through a variety of strategies and activities such as dream work, meditation, journaling, self-reflection, and even body-related practices such as Hatha Yoga, Tai Chi, Aikido, or dance. It is also likely that he or she has sought out and found fellow travelers in the form of friends or even partners on the path of personal growth. He or she is likely to be an intelligent and well educated person, perhaps with an advanced degree. He or she may live an unconventional lifestyle, though this is not necessarily the case, and often has had more cross-cultural experiences than the average person.

This overall picture leads to the conclusion that high levels of personal evolution are earned over time by a sustained commitment. In other words, ego development is not achieved through a single dramatic growth experience, or even multiple experiences, though these may occasionally help.[32]

On the other hand, and perhaps surprisingly, it is sometimes the case that overcoming personal hardships such as the loss of a job, a divorce, or the death of a loved one can actually harden the personality, blocking further growth. It is as if the person says, "I've overcome this great hardship. Now I am *strong* and I will never let anything like this happen to me again!" But this attitude can cut off an openness to new experiences that seems necessary for higher levels of growth to find their footing.

The truth of the matter is that most highly developed persons have lived non-traumatic lives which have not involved emotional or financial hardships, but have been blessed with the freedom and even leisure to pursue their own growth. Along with this they have made it a habit to be open to the opportunities the kosmos has offered them, moving forward rather than taking the safe path of keeping a job or a lifestyle that is conservative, safe, and uninspiring.[33]

A quick note on complexity

In the previous chapter I labored to tie each stage of growth to the cognitive line, especially in terms of Piaget's basic theory of developmental periods. My intention was to make clear the growth of the underlying structure and logic of the mind, as well as the transformations of conscious experience patterned by it. If we stand back and view the stages of growth charted there from infancy to adulthood, we see that one important theme that runs throughout development is a persistent increase in internal complexity which lies inside and powers the growth of the mind. This complexity presents itself in the form of increasingly sophisticated schemas and patterns of schemas all of which constitute a person's mind. In this way our experience of reality is also patterned.

The theme of complexity continues to characterize mental growth, and with it the transformation of experience, as we encounter advanced stages of development. Here it is not so much a matter of becoming smarter or more clever, but of acquiring flexible perspectives that are open to many facets of experience, and with them a growing attainment of creative and supple ways to relate to other people and address the day to day challenges we all face. For those who are interested, I explore this idea in detail in my book *The Radiance of Being*, as well as elsewhere.[34] The point here, however, is that growth at all levels of development is supported, and to a significant degree created, by the blossoming of internal complexity.

The Wilber-Combs lattice

It makes sense that there is a close relationship between the complexity of cognitive structures on the one hand, and ways of experiencing the world on the other. We saw several examples of this in the previous chapter. Table 6.1 illustrated the correspondence between Piaget's stages of cognitive growth and Gebser's structures of consciousness, or worldviews. For instance, preoperational thinking that is characteristic of young childhood is associated with magical thinking, while the concrete operations thinking of later childhood is associated with mythic ideation. Adult formal operations thinking brings with it ordinary adult mental experience.

In fact, we can extend our examination of these ideas to include states and structures that lie beyond the ordinary, conventional, mental level of development, and include the postconventional stages described previously. Wilber and I have attempted to show that these postconventional developmental levels are affiliated with structures of consciousness already well-known in the literature of mystical and wisdom traditions throughout the world.[35] Here, however, we come to a problem.

For the postconventional developmental stages, especially at the advanced levels of the illumined mind and onward, the underlying cognitive structures, or ways of thinking and perceiving, are so intimately associated with particular states of consciousness, and these in turn with traditional realms of being, that it is difficult to tease them apart and understand one without the other. For example, the illumined mind is usually associated with the psychic or lower subtle realm, the intuitive mind with the higher subtle realm, and the overmind mind with the causal realm, and these are also thought of as states of consciousness.

When such states are actually experienced they carry such a palpable sense of reality that it is indeed tempting to conclude that one has been transported to an alternative realm of being, a reality that exists quite independently of human cognitive structures. In this light, the developmental achievement of a particular cognitive structure seems simply a way to access such realms. While it is easy to understand how the magical thinking of the child might create a world of magical experience, it is not so easy to see how the cognitive structure of the intuitive mind could create the subtle realm that Wilber associates with deity mysticism. Or how the cognitive structure of the overmind could create the elevated experience of the causal realm. In fact, these realms are described in ancient traditions, such as Vedanta, as actual planes of being associated with energetic or vibrational sheaths that form part of the invisible energy architecture of the human body.

So the question clarifies itself into this: do we create these realms of experience, these states of consciousness, through our own modes of thinking, that is our cognitive organization, or are they already part of the Kosmos waiting for us to refine our mental instrument sufficiently to detect and experience them? This question comes more into focus when we consider the fact that it is not uncommon for people to experience temporary elevated states of consciousness, or peak experiences, without having first developed the cognitive structures needed to stabilize them through the ordinary process of psychological growth. In other words, even people at lower levels of development such as children have temporary peak experiences, sometimes of advanced mystical states, without giving any evidence of having achieved high levels of cognitive development.

Putting the question differently, do we create advanced states of consciousness *ex nihilo*, through the development of sophisticated cognitive structures, or when we experience them do we somehow enter pre-existing realms of being inaccessible to the ordinary mind? Strangely enough, it seems there is considerable evidence for both views. Research tells us beyond doubt that ordinary people, including children, report temporary peak experiences that fit classical descriptions of the lower and higher subtle realms (nature mysticism and deity mysticism), the causal realm (formless mysticism), and even nondual consciousness.[36] In this vein it is also worth noting that many spiritual practitioners, for example in the Zen Buddhist tradition, are "state trained" (to use Wilber's phrase) to enter alternative realms of consciousness directly from ordinary awareness, bypassing any kind of long-term structural growth process.

The few adequate studies that we have inform us that the highest stages of personal growth involve complex cognitive structures which yield many of the properties of these advanced states of consciousness.[37] So one cannot doubt that, if carried far enough, psychological growth begins to facilitate or even produce the characteristics of higher states of consciousness. For instance, the sense of self becomes permeable and the individual begins to let go of rigid personal boundaries previously maintained by the ego. At the same time there is an expanding sense of affiliation with others and even nonhuman life—a growing compassion for all life.

I am afraid we will not get to the bottom of this question today. For the moment let us consider the nature of consciousness to be like a photon of light. When viewed as a particle it exhibits all the properties of a particle following a specific trajectory, at each moment existing at a single point in space and so on. But when viewed as a wave it exhibits the properties of a wave, for example interacting with other waves by addition or subtraction (interference), spreading out through space, and confined to no single location. In analogous fashion, when states of consciousness are viewed as the product of cognitive structures that grow and mature over time, it is seen that they indeed exhibit properties such as slow maturation that advances and recedes over time—eventually becoming stable and strong. When viewed, however, as pre-existing states it is seen that they exhibit those properties too. The most obvious of these is that they can spontaneously appear full-blown and even unexpectedly in people who in some instances have no psychological preparation for them whatsoever. Here is an example of the latter situation.

John Wren-Lewis spontaneously awoke into a transcendent state of consciousness that was not acquired through any kind of spiritual or other training, but triggered by an overdose of an unknown drug. This occurred in 1993 when he was 60 years old. He and his wife were traveling in Thailand when a stranger offered them toffees as they were getting on a bus. John ate his candy while his wife wisely declined. As it turned out, the candy was laced with a strong dose of drugs. John fell into a coma and was taken to a local hospital. A short time after awakening he began to have unusual experiences. To begin with, the room he was in seemed surprisingly beautiful. He also became aware of blissful feelings of joy, love, and wellbeing. Reflecting on his new experiences he became aware of a deep connection with a formless ground of being just behind the surface of things. In time he came to view his previous state of ordinary consciousness as a "clouded condition" in which he suffered the illusion of being a "separate individual entity over and against everything else."[38] He later stated that it was as if a cataract had been removed from his brain, opening his head to infinity. With occasional fluctuations John has maintained this exceptional state of consciousness continuously since its original awakening.

On the other hand Bernadette Roberts is a living example of a modern mystic, or "contemplative" as she would say, who lives in a continuous transcendent state of nondual awareness that was not spontaneous at all but, rather, the fruit of many years of religious devotion. Roberts grew up in a Catholic family and was drawn to a religious life as a young lady. She entered the Carmelite order in her early teens and soon experienced a spiritual deepening similar to the "dark nights of the soul" described by Saint John of the Cross. During the years that followed she underwent a rich and amazing variety of inner experiences, some ecstatic and some intensely discomforting. She bore all of these in a deep and constant faith in traditional Christian ideals as personified in the lives of the great Catholic saints, especially John of the Cross. Her experiences as well as her religious philosophy are chronicled in her books, such as *The Experience of No-Self: A Contemplative Journey.*[39]

Roberts' struggle through the sometimes agonizing challenges and cleansing flames of personal transformation was informed by her faith in Christ and the Church, but she did not have the benefit of a traditional guide or teacher who was familiar with the stages of psychospiritual growth through which she passed. She was on her own, or perhaps we should say on her own with the inspired guidance of the Holy Spirit. But as we know, inspiration rarely presents us with details on how to proceed. Roberts had to work these out for herself. Her story has something in common with that of the Indian yogi, Gopi Krishna.

As a young man Gopi Krishna pursued a basic meditation practice, but did not have a guru or other traditional guide. Nevertheless, he managed to awaken a powerful spontaneous experience of kundalini that nearly overwhelmed him. In his autobiography, *Kundalini: The Evolutionary Energy in Man*, he wrote,

> Suddenly, with a roar like that of a waterfall, I felt a stream of liquid light entering my brain through the spinal cord.
>
> Entirely unprepared for such a development, I was completely taken by surprise...The illumination grew brighter and brighter, the roaring louder, I experienced a rocking sensation and then felt myself slipping out of my body, entirely enveloped in a halo of light... I felt the point of consciousness that was myself growing wider surrounded by waves of light. ...I was now all consciousness without any outline, without any idea of corporeal appendage, without any feeling or sensation coming from the senses, immersed in a sea of light simultaneously conscious and aware at every point, spread out, as it were, in all directions without any barrier or material obstruction.[40]

This amazing experience was just the first of an odyssey of powerful and often disturbing experiences Gopi Krishna would endure over the course of coming years before finally managing to bring his transformed mind, body, and spirit into a stable and healthy condition. In time Gopi Krishna, who had failed in school as a young man, became a gifted writer and teacher.

Though he did not have the help of a guide or guru during this process, the American psychologist James Hillman points out in his introduction to Gopi Krishna's autobiography that he did have the benefit of a cultural and spiritual tradition that recognized and honored the kinds of powerful transformational experiences he was going through and did not consider him to be disturbed or psychotic.

Unlike Gopi Krishna, who was practicing potent meditation techniques on his own, some student practitioners in time-honored wisdom traditions throughout the world undergo powerful transformative experiences while receiving guidance from their teachers. The journeys of these students are often less traumatic than those experienced by Gopi Krishna and Bernadette Roberts. This is in part because such traditions provide systematic practices that guide the growth of the practitioner step-by-step.[41] It is also because an important role of the teacher or guru is to personally direct and protect the student.

One of my own experiences that illustrates the latter point took place during a short period when I was practicing kundalini yoga as a young man. My teacher, Swami Rama, had given me a series of breath exercises for cleansing which I practiced for several days prior to applying the "breath of fire" designed to awaken the kundalini. After one or two days of the latter a powerful dream came to me in which a large lion had been awakened deep in the earth. Its roar shook the landscape like an earthquake and I realized with fear that if it got out into the open it would be dangerous and impossible to control. Needless to say, I went back to my cleansing exercises which I practiced for several more weeks. Shortly after beginning the breath of fire again I had another dream. In it a large lion was walking in a field not far away, and my teacher was standing nearby. Someone asked me if I was not afraid of the lion. "No," I answered, "It is not dangerous when my teacher is here." Swami Rama, in fact, always maintained that half or more of a student's spiritual work is the responsibility of the teacher. I make no judgment on this, but it does point to the importance of a teacher or guide for helping the student make his or her way forward. During this period of practice I did not experience the dramatic rising of the kundalini up the spinal cord often described by kundalini practitioners. It did seem to me on later reflection, however, that I had been subtly changed into a more complete and effective human being.

But now let us return to states and structures of experience. In particular, consider the situation in which a person experiences a temporary shift of consciousness to one of the higher states, in other words, has a peak experience. As Abraham Maslow discovered long ago, peak experiences are typically temporary, lasting no more than a few minutes to a few hours.[42] Then, like a hot air balloon that soars high into the sky before returning to earth, the peak experience slowly dissipates to be replaced by the same structure of experience the person has been used to all along. Everything returns to normal. The existence of such peak experiences seems consistent with the idea that the people who have them actually enter a different realm of experience rather than somehow undergoing a temporary structural shift in their mental makeup.[43]

We will return to this question shortly, but first let us also take a moment to examine a related question. In particular, how does a person reconcile these temporary experiences with their everyday sense of reality? During such elevated experiences the world may appear quite different than it usually does. For instance, a person may sense a "rightness" to things just the way they are, beyond moral or other kinds of considerations. The American mystic Franklin Merrell-Wolff referred to this attitude as "high indifference." At the same time there may be a sense or perhaps a feeling of unity with all the world, quite opposite of our usual perception that the cosmos is populated by separate people and discrete objects. There may be a realization that everything is subtly mirrored in everything else, like the *Net of Indra*, in which each multifaceted jewel (or pearl in some versions) is reflected simultaneously in all the others. Beyond this, there may be a deepened sense of reality as if seeing the world properly for the first time. Other qualities of peak experiences could be listed, but the point is that for most people these are not usual ways of perceiving or thinking. How then does a person reconcile this temporary but dramatically altered reality with their normal sense of things?

Psychologists tell us it is uncomfortable to hold two conflicting views at the same time. The term for this is *cognitive dissonance*. When it occurs, people go out of their way to eliminate one view or the other. Let's say John, for example, has been lucky in a lottery drawing at the local mall where he had purchased some tickets to help support the Girl Scouts and won himself a new Ford sedan. In the past he was not enthusiastic about Fords. In fact he had avoided purchasing them. Now, as he drives his new car around town, sniffs the scent of the new upholstery and discovers how good his favorite stations sound on the radio, he becomes increasingly convinced that he has won an excellent car! If he doesn't have too much trouble with it he may even buy another for his daughter who will soon be graduating from high school. As his enthusiasm increases he may go so far as to get himself a bumper sticker that boldly states, "I would rather tow a Ford than drive a Chevrolet!" John is a perfect example of cognitive dissonance at work. People change their attitudes and their behaviors to resolve a conflict between beliefs, perceptions, or behaviors.

To highlight the question of how someone might reconcile the disparities between an altered state of consciousness and their ordinary sense of reality, let us take an extreme case. Suppose while fiddling with his new car's radio John manages to drive off the road and down a cliff, in the bargain treating himself to a near-death experience. During this experience he seems to pass through a long tunnel before arriving on the other side in a field of light where he senses a number of other presences. Some of these have the familiar feel of deceased relatives. One, however, appears to be a being of power and light that leads John to review the details of his life. Not long into this process, however, he feels something tugging at him from behind and almost instantly he wakes up in considerable pain in the intensive care ward of a nearby hospital. Now, what is he likely to tell people about this experience?

Research informs us that if John is a practical, no-nonsense, kind of guy, he may not tell anyone about this experience at all, chalking it up to some sort of strange trauma-induced dream. It is surprising how many people do exactly the same thing with peak experiences. They simply hide them away, in some cases even finding them frightening to think about. But let's suppose that John is a traditionally religious man. Maybe he was raised in a devout Catholic family where the conventional teachings of the church were taken literally, seriously, and without question. In this case, John may report that he traveled to heaven where he met several of his deceased relatives and was confronted by Jesus Christ. His family members may believe him, or, for one reason or another, try to convince him that this experience was delusional or even the work of the devil.

People have similar reactions to peak experiences. If they are religious people they may interpret peak experiences as divine grace by which they have come near to God or Christ (or angels, etc.). In other words, they may believe they have had a *religious* experience as understood in the terms of their own faith. In this case they might seek a priest or minister to help sort out what happened to them. On the other hand if they have open-minded scientific attitudes toward life they might have read about near-death experiences and recognize the fact that they have had one. They might then reflect on what this experience says in terms of the greater meaning of life, and they may seek out others who have had similar experiences. They may feel thankful to have had a momentary glimpse of a deeper order of reality that they had not previously known.

Such examples demonstrate that different people have different ways of understanding unusual experiences. Each tends to interpret their experience in the ways they already understand the world. But let us recall that these ways of understanding the world are not independent of that person's developmental structure. In fact, they are very much a product of these structures. The preoperational child, for example, understands the world in terms of magical thinking. Similarly, the adult who still thinks in magical terms is likely to hold religious beliefs that emphasize magic. As Wilber points out, such a person may frame their religious beliefs in terms of Christ the healer and miracle worker.[44] This person is also likely to understand a peak experience, say a brief flight into the subtle realm, in magical terms: a child reporting voices of fairies, an adult the songs of angels. An adult who thinks in concrete operations terms— Gebser's mythic mind—tends to seek absolute truth and may discover in a brief peak experience a window into the true and final nature of reality. An adult at the mental or rational stage of cognitive development might look in wonder at how deeply and how logically connected all aspects of the world can be. Such perceptions lie just on the edge of the next developmental stage of pluralism, which emphasizes systems thinking, disclosing a vision of the interconnectedness of all biological life and the ecological world.

For the time being let us take the view that peak experiences such as those described above are actual transports into alternative realms of experience, or realms of being if one prefers, such as those described in the ancient Vedanta philosophy. We are already familiar with these realms and recall that they are found in one form or another in many wisdom traditions throughout the world. The most basic division of these realms includes gross or material, subtle, causal, and nondual as described earlier in the chapter. Now add to this the fact that each of these realms can be experienced at virtually any stage of cognitive development and we have the basis of a matrix, or lattice, that illustrates the richness and range of experiential possibilities in terms of the ways that peak experiences might be experienced and interpreted.

Levels[1]/Realms[2]	Gross	Psychic[3]	Subtle	Causal	Nondual[4]
Nondual[4] (Supermind)	--	--	--	--	--
Causal (Causal)	--	--	--	--	--
Subtle (higher Subtle)	--	--	--	--	--
Psychic[3] (lower Subtle)	--	--	--	--	--
Integral or Vision Logic (systems thinking)	--	--	--	--	--
Formal Operations	--	--	--	--	--
Concrete Operations	--	--	--	--	--
Early Concrete Operations	--	--	--	--	--
Preoperational	--	--	--	--	--
Sensorimotor	--	--	--	--	--

Table 7.2: A Wilber-Combs Lattice.
[1]Levels of development. Terms are based on a number of developmental systems.[45]
[2]Realms of being. These may be thought of as actual realms of being, or states of consciousness that carry a strong sense of reality.
[3]Also termed lower subtle.
[4]Ever-present ordinary mind; the direct experience of the nondual ground.

In Table 7.2 we see developmental stages on the left and the traditional realms of experience across the top. We can imagine that anyone at virtually any stage of development can have a peak experience at any of the levels indicated across the top. This lattice includes ten developmental levels and five traditional states of experience (or realms of being), giving a total of 50 different combinations each of which represents its own discrete way of experiencing and understanding the world.

Since the "higher" or more subtle realms of experience are often interpreted in religious terms, it is tempting to consider the possibilities represented in Table 7.2 from a spiritual perspective as well. Indeed, Wilber has done exactly this in Table 7.3.

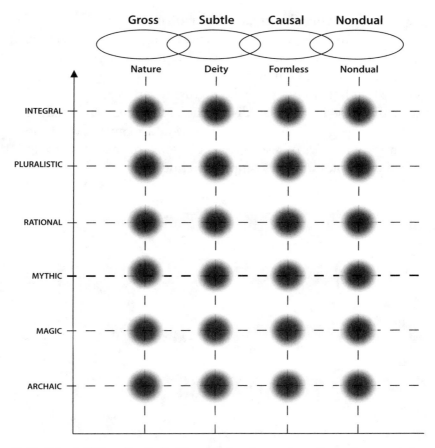

Table 7.3: A Wilber–Combs Lattice showing four realms of experience and six developmental stages.[46]

In this table we find six developmental stages on the left, each labeled in terms of Jean Gebser's worldviews (or structures of conscious), and the four basic realms of experience (or being) across the top. To the latter Wilber has superimposed the four basic forms of mysticism that emerge from the study of wisdom traditions worldwide: nature mysticism, deity mysticism, formless mysticism, and nondual awareness. He describes these in detail in several of his books. The lattice itself presents his integration of the religious scholarship of James Fowler,[47] who carefully studied the historical and personal stages of religious development, and

Evelyn Underhill, the great scholar of mysticism. Each of the entries in this table represents an entire religious perspective, just as each of the 50 entries in Table 7.2 represents a particular way of experiencing oneself and the world.

Other lattices might be drawn that illustrate the possibilities of experience in areas as diverse as art, philosophy, medicine, and psychology. To delve into these would require several more volumes, and years of research. So I leave it for the future to flesh out these topics in their complete richness.

8. Horizontal and Vertical Evolution of Consciousness

> To exist is to change, to change is to mature, to mature is to go on creating oneself endlessly.
>
> The eye sees only what the mind is prepared to comprehend.
>
> *Henri Bergson*

The idea that consciousness, or experience, has evolved and may continue to evolve through time and history has been expressed in one way or another by many philosophers and pioneers of the inner life. Often this notion is associated with God or some form of divine spirit.[1] Some of the most important pioneers of our understanding of the evolution of consciousness are noted below.

Here I note that much of the following discussion derives from Western cultural history.

Georg Wilhelm Hegel

The first and in some ways most influential Western philosopher to think about the evolution of consciousness was Georg Wilhelm Hegel who, writing at the beginning of the nineteenth century, envisioned history as the story of the struggle of the divine spirit towards self-manifestation. He thought of mind, spirit, and consciousness—viewing the three as a unity—as evolving from primitive sense-perception through various forms including art, religion, and philosophy towards absolute knowledge that understands its own evolutionary reality. Put simply, he believed that humankind is the vehicle though which the divine spirit finds its own realization.

Henri Bergson and Teilhard de Chardin

Another influential thinker, though less concerned with the divine and more interested in the evolution of consciousness itself, was the turn-of-the-century French philosopher Henri Bergson. Introduced to American readers with great enthusiasm by no less than William James, Bergson advocated an evolutionary view of biological life in general, picturing consciousness as a kind of pressure struggling toward increasing expression and freedom through evolutionary growth. He wrote,

> Consciousness, even in the most rudimentary animal, covers by right an enormous field, but is compressed in fact in a kind of vise: each advance of the nervous centers, by giving the organism a choice between a larger number of actions, calls forth the potentialities that are capable of surrounding the real, thus opening the vise wider and allowing consciousness to pass more freely.[2]

Bergson saw consciousness as the *raison d'etre* for all life, and the human being its highest evolutionary expression. Now, such ideas may seem quaint or even offensive to today's readers. But in the intellectual climate of turn-of-the-century Europe and America they were very popular, representing a resolution of the paradox presented by the huge success of human reason as seen in the industrial revolution, and the newly coined Darwinian discovery that the human being is but an animal among animals. For Bergson we are the vehicles through which consciousness finds its highest and most successful expression. He even suggested that humankind may be the very reason for life on Earth.

Bergson was enormously popular with European and American intellectual audiences. His book, *Creative Evolution*, was printed in more than 20 languages and his lectures in Paris at the *Collège de France* were so crowded that a larger auditorium had to be found which, again, overflowed. After World War I, however, philosophy around the world became much less grandiose and optimistic, giving way to an almost universal austerity as seen in British analytic philosophy and the Viennese movement of logical positivism, which by mid-century dominated scientific thought in virtually every field. Nevertheless, Bergson had one brilliant successor in the person of a French Jesuit priest by the name of Père Teilhard de Chardin. The latter's life work remained in obscurity, under the censorship of the church, until near his death in 1955 when for a short time he was widely read and enthusiastically discussed. Today the name of Teilhard de Chardin is still frequently mentioned and, indeed, is more familiar to most ears than that of his renowned predecessor.

Teilhard de Chardin's writings, most notably *The Phenomenon of Man,*[3] reflect many of Bergson's earlier notions about the position of consciousness as central to evolution both in humankind and other species. He reiterated Bergson's idea that consciousness strives in the course of evolution to achieve ever greater freedom of expression through increasingly complex supporting structures such as the human nervous system. In Teilhard de Chardin one also finds a tincture of Hegel's notion of evolution as an expression of the divine striving for manifestation in human experience. For Teilhard de Chardin, however, consciousness is pulled forward toward a kind of universal synthesis in the formation of a higher principle he termed the Omega Point. The latter is a mystical fusion of human consciousness brought about by a transcendence of the individual into a greater unity though the action of love.

It is worth noting that Teilhard de Chardin's Omega Point is more than an abstraction. Once formed it becomes more like a living being, or even a divine presence that can influence the individual lives that comprise it. Much as the brain influences the activities of the individual nerve cells of which it is formed the Omega Point may exert a certain "gravity," or pull, backwards through time, actually drawing us towards its future formation. Thus, in many ways it is like a divine being. Its actual relationship to the traditional Christian God was unclear in Teilhard de

Chardin's writings, however, and as you can imagine this ambiguity was not especially popular with conservative factions in the Catholic Church.

Teilhard de Chardin's Omega Point continues to be a topic of discussion and inspiration though few contemporary theologians or philosophers take it entirely seriously. Nevertheless, the possibility of some kind of melding together of the many separate lights of human consciousness is not too far afield from contemporary explorations into the evolutionary possibility of shared intelligence, a notion to which we will return near the end of the chapter.

Sri Aurobindo

Another pioneer of the evolution of consciousness was the Indian sage and yogi, Aurobindo Akroyd Ghose, or as the world now knows him, Sri Aurobindo. Having spent much of his youth in England where he grew up and received a Cambridge education, he returned to India as an adult and became a significant figure in India's struggle for freedom from England. In 1908 he was arrested on charges of sedition and held for an entire year in solitary confinement before being acquitted. This was a critical year for Sri Aurobindo's transformation into a great yogi, as he spent much of it deeply immersed in spiritual contemplation. Not long after being released, however, he sensed the British were planning to arrest him again and he immediately traveled out of their jurisdiction to French India where he began a new life as a yogi and spiritual philosopher. During the years that followed he wrote prodigiously on yoga, spirituality, and the evolution of consciousness. He died in 1950, but his partner, Mirra Alfassa, known to the world as The Mother, continued the work he had started until her own passing in 1973.

Sri Aurobindo's evolutionary philosophy and his accompanying *Integral Yoga* represent a complex set of ideas and practices still very much alive today. The ashram that he and The Mother founded in Pondicherry remains an active center of spiritual scholarship and practice, and the nearby community of

Auroville is a vigorous embodiment of the spiritual and practical philosophies Sri Aurobindo and The Mother created during their lifetimes. Globally, Sri Aurobindo's ideas are probably more widely-discussed and implemented today than even during his own lifetime or that of The Mother.

Sri Aurobindo's Integral Yoga

Sri Aurobindo and The Mother were deeply committed to an evolutionary philosophy and practice that is both traditional and at the same time completely original. It is traditional in that it draws on the ancient Indian philosophy of Vedanta and in particular the ascending levels of being identified in Vedanta, which also represent "vehicles" or nested sheaths that surround the individual Self or Atman. We are already familiar with a slightly less-detailed version of this system from the previous chapter. As shown in Table 8.1, these begin with the physical body itself and are said to include the pranic or energy sheath, the mental sheath, the subtle sheath, and the causal sheath, leading toward the highest level of supramental consciousness not shown in the table because it is not a sheath or level at all but beyond and containing these. As in the previous chapter, the pranic and mental levels are sometimes combined as the "lower subtle," contrasted with the "higher subtle," or subtle proper, just beneath the causal realm.

Anandamaya kosha	(sheath of bliss)	causal body
Vijnanamaya kosha	(intellect)	subtle body
Manomaya kosha	(mental sheath)	mental body
Pranamaya kosha	(energy sheath)	pranic body
Annamaya kosha	(food sheath)	physical body

Table 8.1. The sheaths (koshas) of Vedanta that surround the Self.

Integral Yoga is nontraditional, not because it attempts to penetrate these realms, as do most forms of yoga, but because it views yogic transformations as an evolutionary process. In Sri Aurobindo's words:

> In my explanation of the universe I have put forward this cardinal fact of a spiritual evolution as the meaning of our existence here. It is a series of ascents from the physical being and consciousness to the vital, the being dominated by the life-self, thence to the mental being realized in the fully developed man and thence into the perfect consciousness which is beyond the mental.[4]

In Sri Aurobindo's terms the "vital" refers to the pranic or energy sheath, the "mental" to the mental sheath, and perfect consciousness to the supramental, beyond all levels or vehicles. One difference between Integral Yoga and traditional yogic schools is that its aim is not to release the practitioner from the pull of the physical but rather to integrate all levels of the being into a harmonious whole. This is the meaning of the term *integral*, in Integral Yoga, and is understood as a purifying process that builds on the foundation of the physical world and the subtle realms associated with it. Beyond Integral Yoga, however, comes an even more advanced Supramental Yoga for those few practitioners who have advanced to the highest stages of yogic achievement. In the latter, one strives to actually draw down the transcendent energies and knowledge (*gnosis*) of the spiritual kosmos, rooted above in the divine and which have never been shrouded in matter. Ideally, taking this process to its conclusion means to open the mental and physical to the decent of this transforming energy right down to the atoms of the physical body.

In their own practice Sri Aurobindo and The Mother worked diligently to embody this transformation, thus "opening a channel" for the transformation of others as well. It is said among their contemporary followers that Sri Aurobindo did not completely achieve this transformation during his lifetime but that The Mother went further during the 23 years she lived after his passing. Whether she actually completed the perfect evolutionary transformation is, however, an open question. Perhaps the most important point for our purposes is that Sri Aurobindo and The Mother both conceived of personal transformation in terms of the evolution of mind, body, and spirit. In fact, both Sri Aurobindo and The Mother considered the contemporary human to be only a step along a continuing evolutionary trajectory and not the final goal. In this sense they shared with Teilhard de Chardin a vision of future evolution that included a much-expanded role of the spirit.

Jean Gebser

We are already familiar with Jean Gebser's evolutionary view of structures of consciousness—the archaic, magic, mythic, mental, and integral—from Chapter 6, so I will not go into details about them again here. But let us take a moment to consider Gebser's underlying view of the evolutionary process itself. Basically, Gebser seems to have been a modern Neoplatonist. The central ideal of the ancient mystical philosophy of Neoplatonism, surprisingly similar to that found in Hindu thought, was that the highest principle of creation, the *One*, overflows in its own richness, cascading down to create the various levels of being that lead ultimately toward matter.[5] Basic to Gebser's thinking was the idea of the *Origin* which, like the Neoplatonic One, plays the role of the central creative principle of life and the kosmos. Each evolutionary transformation, each new structure of consciousness, was seen by Gebser not as emerging into the human experience *ex nihilo*, nor as the product of Darwinian natural selection, but as the emergence of another aspect of the Origin that had not before been seen.

I have examined these ideas in detail elsewhere.[6] The point here is that Gebser, like Sri Aurobindo, saw the historically unfolding structures of consciousness as emerging according to a pre-established agenda. Now, there are two important observations I would like to make about this. The first is that such a view allows no latitude for fundamental creativity. Rather, in each instance the forward progression of consciousness is seen as the unfurling of a predetermined pattern. Perhaps there is room for creativity in the expression of the details, but this basic notion of evolution is quite unlike modern ideas of evolution that emphasize unpredictable originality in each new phase of development. This, of course, does not mean that Gebser or Sri Aurobindo were wrong. It only means that they used the term "evolution" differently than do most contemporary writers. In fact, Gebser did not use the term at all because he objected to the way it had been employed to justify racial and ethnic abuses by the Social Darwinists.[7] This, plus the fact that he did not believe the more recent structures of consciousness to be superior to earlier ones, at least not prior to the advent of the integral structure of consciousness.

A second and more pressing point here is that the evolutionary agendas of Sri Aurobindo and Gebser, like Hegel, Bergson, and Teilhard de Chardin before them, regarded the progression of consciousness in terms of intensity or spiritual elevation. Intensity in that each depicted this progress in one sense or another as an increasingly direct, luminous, and powerful expression of a deeper truth. And elevation in the sense that each strove for increasingly direct expressions of the highest forms of the spirit, however that form is conceived. In each instance we find an emphasis on *ascent*, which I will refer to here as *vertical evolution*. In the following section I will introduce the alternative concept of *horizontal evolution*.

Horizontal Evolution

The idea of *horizontal evolution* is suggested by the fact that over the course of human history there have appeared an increasing number of perspectives through which we human beings have come to experience the Kosmos. In plain English, the number of points of view from which a modern person can see and understand the world is much greater than those available to our ancestors. Naturally, as more perspectives have become possible the net sum of human experience has become richer. Let me explain by starting with a simple and dramatic example.

Consider the somewhat startling fact that the distinction we commonly make between our "inner" perspective of thoughts, memories, and feelings, and our "outer" perspective of the external world, in other words the basic division of the kosmos into Wilber's left and right quadrants, has not always been with us. For example, ancient philosophers and writers virtually never gave attention to the presence of any kind of internal subjective actor as the owner of their thoughts, memories, and feelings. In the *Iliad* and the *Odyssey* everything that we would today attribute to the inner life comes from the outside, often through the mouths of gods or goddesses.

For instance, Odysseus' son Telemachus travels from the island kingdom of Ithaca to Sparta on mainland Greece to seek from dead Agamemnon's brother Menelaus knowledge of his long-absent father. During his visit he is awakened in the night by a sudden urgency to return to Ithaca, there to deal with the suitors who have gathered around his mother, Penelope. The key point here is that he did not wake up at three in the morning with a worried sense that something was wrong at home, a sense powerful enough to drive him immediately to gather his men and set sail. Rather, he was awakened by the goddess Athena who warned him of trouble at home and who urged him to return at once.

Ancient tales from all around the world include such exchanges between human beings and gods or goddesses. This, plus the absence of inner dialogue, led psychologist Julian Jaynes in 1976 to publish his now famous book, *The Origin of Consciousness in the Breakdown of the Bicameral Mind*,[8] in which he argued that the voices heard by ancients were actually projected hallucinations of the right hemisphere of the brain. This idea holds little credibility today, but we are still left with the enigma of why intelligent men from Plato to Marcus Aurelius failed to identify an inner actor as the source of their thoughts. A notable exception near the end of the Roman Empire was Saint

Augustine of Hippo, whose inwardly-centered *Confessions* seem amazingly familiar to the modern mind.

After the fall of the Roman Empire in the West around end of the fifth century c.e., personal diaries and journals disappeared entirely and did not again reflect the presence of inner subjective actors until the rise of the Italian Renaissance. During the Middle Ages many books were written on cooking, etiquette, marriage, morals, and dying, but virtually no author anguished over an inner person in the grips of anger, guilt, fear, or obligation. Historian Morris Berman[9] notes that it is almost as if people during these times were like robots, living out automated social roles with little or no reflection on what life meant to them personally. This absence of self-reflection is illustrated quite literally by the virtual absence of mirrors and a lack of concern over ordinary privacy. The latter is seen in the common absence of separate bedrooms for the nobility in palaces of the period.[10]

At the beginning of the Italian Renaissance and most notably in the fourteenth-century journals of Petrarch[11] we find a return of self-reflection that soon began to spread. It was not until the publication of Descartes' *Meditations on First Philosophy* in 1641, however, that the distinction between an inner world of thought and feeling and an outer world of physical objects and objective reality were systematically defined and contrasted. For this reason Descartes is sometimes said to have "invented" the modern notion of consciousness as an inner dimension of experience.

With Descartes we can clearly say that the world of human experience had become divided into two realms, or two perspectives, an inner perspective and an outer perspective. This is an important instance of the lateral evolution of consciousness, one in which a bifurcation in perspective has created two worlds of experience out of one original world.

Let's look a bit more closely at exactly what this all means. Recall the example of Telemachus from the *Odyssey*. A completely realistic interpretation of how Telemachus came to leave Sparta in the middle of the night[12] is that he awoke, as many of us do from time to time, at three in the morning worrying about the uncertainties of his life. In his case the biggest worry he had was that the mob of suitors gathering about his mother would gang up on him and kill him so that one of them could marry Penelope and, in Odysseus' absence, declare himself the king of Ithaca. This is enough to make any sound minded young man gather together his faithful friends and head for home as quickly as possible. You or I would say, "I got worried in the middle of the night and decided I had better head for home." But Telemachus did not see it this way because he did not distinguish between inner anguish and outer warnings of danger. So he responded to his sense of urgency by telling himself that Athena was directing him to return home.

Now let us take an example closer to home. Suppose you go for a walk in the forest and find yourself confronted by a bear! Your immediate perception is that the bear is dangerous and frightening. That is, you experience the qualities of danger and threat to reside in the bear. In this way they are experienced outside yourself as qualities inherent in the bear. But wait. Suddenly you notice that this animal is not a bear at all but a huge friendly Saint Bernard dog. You feel silly and realize on reflection that your fear resided in yourself all along and not in the animal. Freed of the fear of being attacked by a bear, you are able to shift your perspective to your inner experience and see that the fear was your own all the time. This is a shift many modern adults can make, but was probably not available to ancient people any more than it is available to children today, who would simply experience the animal, once a bear and now a dog, as no longer frightening.

To distinguish the inside from the outside can be a tricky business. Much of the psychology developed by Sigmund Freud, Carl Jung, and others deals with aspects of the unconscious that do not seem to be located inside of us at all, but outside of ourselves as projections encountered in the world of objective reality. Such projections make up much of the fabric of our personal lives in terms of our loves, hates, fears, desires, and so on. For instance, this man or woman is romantically or sexually attractive, this one is frightening, and another is wise or powerful. What we see in others often comes from deep within ourselves, returning to us in the form of perceptions of external reality. A great deal has been written about all this so I will not go into it further, but it is worth noting that to become a fully healthy and conscious person we must learn to deal with these unconscious projections that so profoundly color our experience of others.

Understanding the Zones

Let us further pursue this topic of perspectives by noting the obvious fact that without an inside there can be no outside, and without an outside there can be no inside. That is, one cannot reflect on the nature of one's inner feelings or one's soul unless these are experienced as lying on the inside of an outside. Thus, before the world of experience was cleaved into an inside and an outside the locations of emotions, feelings, desires, and so on, were simply in the world and not specifically in the person. To put it more accurately, they simply existed independently of an inside or an outside. A man might see a woman as desirable, a lion as frightening, or a fine horse as exhilarating, understanding these feelings simply as the way things *are* rather than recognizing them as inner feelings.

Reflecting on this situation we realize that to observe the inner movement of our own thoughts and feelings we must have a place to stand, a perspective that lends us the necessary objectivity to see our own inner stream of experience. Wilber refers to the inner experience itself as Zone 1, and the objective perspective from which it can be observed as Zone 2. From Zone 2 we get "the look of the feel" as he calls it. Descartes, for instance, had to adopt a Zone 2 perspective to "objectively" view the realities of Zone 1 and at the same time appreciate their subjectivity. Zone 1, then, refers to actual qualities of thought and feeling, while Zone 2 is the objective stance from which these can be witnessed. Note, however, that both Zones 1 and

2 are in Wilber's upper left quadrant, meaning that they both concern interior experience.

Interestingly, the relationship of Zone 2 to Zone 1 mirrors a larger relationship between the left and right quadrants. It is only from the view of inner experience that objective outer experience solidifies into the concrete objective world. It is not surprising, then, that materialism, even in the physical sciences, appeared full-blown only after Descartes created the division of the kosmos into an inside, or "consciousness," and an outside, or matter. Hence, Descartes, and subsequently Newton, were absolute materialists where the physical world was concerned, believing in a theory of atoms by which tiny solid particles interact and stick together because they are covered with little hooked bristles like nettles or Velcro. As a curious aside, Newton was deeply disturbed by the obvious reality of gravity, a force that acted at a distance, which he himself had mathematically mapped but could never reconcile with his ideas about the hard material nature of physical reality.

Materialistic science became widely accepted with the advent of the seventeenth century *Age of Reason*, at least in part because the physical world had acquired a new objectivity when placed beside Descartes' recently discovered inner reality. In surprising contrast, it was not for another 200 years that the dialectic between the inner and outer aspects of matter came onto the scene and scientists began to look into the interior of matter itself. Even today the notion of an inner aspect to a material process or object is a bit of a conundrum, so let's take a moment and look more closely at this idea. Recall that everything in the right quadrants is outside of subjectivity and part of the objective or "outer" world. This includes everything from rocks to rabbits[13] to thunderstorms. So what could the inside of the outside mean in a completely right quadrant, non-conscious, and objective frame of reference? Since it is exterior and not interior to conscious experience it must be discovered by implication rather than by direct awareness. In the case of science, such implications will usually be conceptual, often based on logic or mathematics.

One common example is the program at the working core of a computer (not the wires and diodes which, while inside the console, are "outside" in terms of the material world). Another example is the inner structure of matter.

In 1925 while vacationing on the treeless island of Helgoland, where he enjoyed a thankful respite from a severe attack of hay fever, the brilliant young mathematician Werner Heisenberg worked out the matrix algebra that would become foundational to the newly emerging field of quantum mechanics. Of course quantum mechanics deals for the most part with subatomic realities, many aspects of which concern the *insides* of even the smallest particles heretofore known. But at this point in history conceptual interiors of objective exteriors were not yet well crystallized in human experience. Indeed, almost immediately the Danish physicist Niels Bohr developed an objective "Copenhagen Interpretation" of quantum mechanics which became widely accepted and, in a nutshell, stated that the strange events depicted in the mathematics of quantum mechanics should be taken only as predictive of concrete facts in the laboratory—meter readings and the like—and not as representing actual realities interior to matter. This interpretation was consistent with the prevalent philosophy of Logical Positivism, which claimed that all scientific statements must be understood strictly in terms of objective observations. In other words, the mathematics of quantum mechanics are simply guidelines to get the researcher from initial sets of operations in the laboratory to final sets of instrument readings. The mathematical descriptions of strange events between the inputs and outputs mean nothing in themselves.

It was not until roughly the 1960s that physicists, mathematicians, and philosophers, began to revisit the question of quantum mechanics with an eye to the possibility that the mathematics might actually be describing something real beyond experimental outcomes. When this happened the top blew off the whole field and physicists and philosophers began to examine the deep mysteries it held. String Theory is one of the recent products of this examination, and at the time of this writing is often criticized as offering no testable laboratory implications whatsoever! In other words, it is only about the inside of matter and has no outside parts at all, thus giving virtually no testable implications in the laboratory. It is the very nemesis of Logical Positivism.

In the above examples we see that during the twentieth century physics has benefited by increasingly flexible perspectives into the inner nature of matter. Many other fields have experienced similar transformations in the perspectives from which their subject matter is viewed. One way to understand these transformations is in terms of the horizontal evolution of consciousness. We will soon examine this idea in more detail, but first we must become familiar with the notion of zones or perspectives. Originally described by Ken Wilber,[14] these will be helpful for understanding horizontal evolution.

The Eight Perspectives – Moving Horizontally Through Experience

The basic idea here is that while experience has a vertical dimension set by a person's developmental stage, it also has a horizontal dimension represented by the number of perspectives available to that person. Here we are talking about a kind of experiential landscape that maps the various ways persons can understand themselves and their surrounding world.

Let's begin by introducing a more complete set of perspectives as we understand them today.[15] In doing so it is helpful to keep in mind the basic four quadrant system of the AQAL model. Again, the two quadrants on the left represent interior or subjective reality while the two on the right represent external or objective reality. Likewise, the two upper quadrants represent single occasions of objects or events while the two lower quadrants represent plural occasions. All this is familiar.

Now we add the notion that each quadrant contains its own unique interior and exterior. In the UL quadrant this division gives us Zone 1 and Zone 2 with which we are already acquainted. Recall that Zone 1 represents a person's subjective flow of experience while Zone 2 steps back to observe the events of Zone 1 yielding what Wilber calls "the look of the feel."

Moving on to the LL quadrant we have Zone 3 on the inside, which stands for intersubjectivity or shared experience, and on the outside we have Zone 4, which stands for the "external" or objective view of shared experience as seen from a collective outside—in other words, something like the shared view of a shared experience.

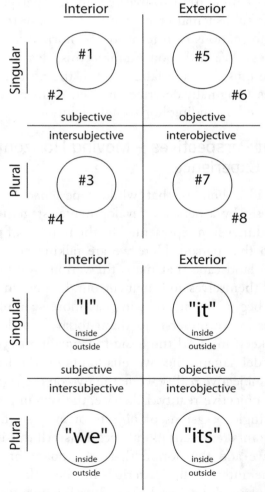

Figure 8.1. Each Quadrant Contains an Inner and Outer Perspective or Zone.[16]

A key point here is that each Zone is both a perspective and at the same time a realm of experience. To clarify this let us note that all experience is grounded in one perspective or another. Flipping this idea over we note that none of our experiences come from nowhere.[17]

Imagine, for instance, that you are enjoying a dinner with friends. The white wine and red snapper are excellent, and you find yourself basking in the warmth of your friends' company. The taste of the wine and the fish, as well as the feelings of friendship are all realities of your Zone 1 perspective. If, however, you pause to consider your pleasure, you are shifting to Zone 2, also a subjective state but with an objective detachment from the flow of "raw" experience that is the reality of the Zone 1. Notice also the almost palpable sense of shared feelings among good friends that cannot be reduced to a collection of individual experiences in each person's Zone 1. This shared sense of friendship is a Zone 3 experience: the sense of being together and what this feels like as a group. You might point this feeling out to the others who may comment on it, sharing their own reflections on the group experience. The "objective" sharing of observations about the group experience is made from Zone 4. Interestingly, too much shared reflection of this type can sometimes have an adverse effect on the quality of the original Zone 3 experience. In other instances, especially when the members of the group feel emotionally close, such sharing can actually heighten the intensity of shared feelings as sometimes occurs between lovers.

Now, let us keep the above example in mind as we continue on to the UR and finally to the LR quadrants where we encounter the four Zones 5, 6, 7, and 8. Touring through these zones we can, for example, see each of our friends simply as physical bodies. This is the Zone 6 perspective. It is the basis of historical behaviorism. Each of our friends' bodies is "behaving", i.e., producing physical movements and sounds that can be recorded and observed objectively. Indeed, all this reminds us of the meaning of the word "objective" as it is used in traditional science: "to be like an object;" material, and visible to anyone who chooses to look.[18] As we have seen, the materialistic science of the *Age of Reason* was based almost entirely on the Zone 6 perspective, according to which the material world is viewed from the outside. Knowledge of interiors does not exist for this zone, so objective knowledge of actual physical interiors, such as the internal organs of the human body, has to be gained by making interiors exterior. Thus it is not surprising that modern scientific knowledge of the human body began historically with the dissection of cadavers, hence rendering the interior exterior. In a different example, the mathematics that comprised Newton's celestial mechanics dealt with solid exterior objects whose interiors were no more than sources of mass and velocity. As we noted above, it was much later that Heisenberg along with other physicists of his generation first developed a science of the interior of matter from the perspective of Zone 5.

Returning to our dinner group, if we were cognitive psychologists we might be interested in the underlying mental processes of these dinner table companions. Many of these processes are unconscious, or perhaps it would be clearer to say they are outside of Zone 1. Examples include the more or less effortless access to personal memories that we take for granted during ordinary conversation, and our easy implementation of complex grammatical conventions during speech. The rules by which such processes are carried out are certainly interior to each of us, but are not to be found by self-reflection. They are studied by cognitive psychologists as one would study a computer program for which one does not have a manual. In other words, by trial and error, or systematically by experiments in the laboratory.

In the latter case, that is, in the case of a scientific experiment, a person might be asked to call to mind various names or facts while a researcher notes the speed of recall. In this case it will be found that memory is quicker and easier if we stick to names or facts about a single topic. Examples include types of seafood, names of actors, breeds of dogs, and so on. If we are forced to jump from one topic to another, however, memory becomes more labored. For instance, it is hard to turn suddenly from a conversation about dogs to one about types of flowers without a few moments to reorient. This becomes more apparent if you know a good bit about these topics. All this tells cognitive psychologists that memory seems to be organized into networks by topic, and also that we can "activate" these networks if we "warm up" with a little practice, talking or thinking about a topic ahead of time. This makes its memory network easier to access. College professors often find that relevant facts come easily to mind in the midst of a lecture, but a question asked in a local café about the same topic can send them on a fishing trip through their own memory. Note that memories are experienced in Zone 1, that is, they are conscious; but the processes that underlie the search and retrieval of memories are not conscious. They are examples of Zone 5 processes not open to Zone 1 experience or Zone 2 observation.

It will come as no surprise that brain scientists, like cognitive psychologists, are also interested in Zone 5 processes. For example, what are the patterns of brain activity that encode sound and light to give us the experience of hearing and seeing? What kinds of brain processes underlie learning and how do these differ, say, in the acquisition of new factual information, novel ideas, or new motor skills? All this has to do with the internal activity patterns of the brain and represents a Zone 5 approach to their understanding, not unlike the way physicists and engineers understand the processes in the silicon hardware that form the basis of the operation of a desktop computer.[19]

But let's return to our dinner friends. Yet another point of view might find us looking at our group as a single set of interacting individuals who make up a small society. This way we see them as an interacting system that might be mapped in terms of the exchange of communication between its members. In this way we would be taking a Zone 8 perspective, that is, looking objectively at the external appearance or dynamics of the group as a physical system. If we probe the internal dynamics of this system, however, we would be moving into a Zone 7 perspective. For example, we might be interested in the structure or dynamics of the conversation itself—the pattern it exhibits in time and space and its self-organizing properties—regardless of who is speaking or the topic of conversation. This Zone 7 perspective is the inside of the objective organization or system which is the group of dinner companions viewed in an objective or LR quadrant way.

Now, here's the thing. *All of our conscious experience flows through these eight zones.* In other words, everything we experience is experienced in one way or another through some combination of these perspectives. Put differently, each instance of our experience is directed toward something on the inside of us (left quadrants) or something on the outside of us (right quadrants). At the same time, each concerns something singular (upper quadrants) or something plural (lower quadrants). And for each of these four possibilities there is an inside view and an outside view, giving eight views, or perspectives, in all. Together these eight Zones embrace our entire spectrum of conscious experience.

Now, this is where it starts getting interesting. Each of these perspectives, or zones, amounts to a unique way of perceiving the world with its own opportunities for knowledge and action. As we have seen, for instance, seventeenth century Newtonian physics, with its emphasis on the dynamics of individual bodies and their interactions is an example of Zone 6, the outside view of the material objects of the outside world. Interestingly, if three or more bodies are included in the problem it has no solution in Newton's system and we must wait until the end of the nineteenth century for the correct approach to appear in the mathematics of Henri Poincaré. The latter moved the problem from the UR quadrant to the LR quadrant and in doing so created the mathematical foundations for what would later become known as chaos theory.

Not surprisingly, Zone 6 art produces realism, as seen in Edouard Manet's celebrated 1863 painting of the reclining nude, *Olympia*, rendering her as material flesh before the eye of the viewer. This was a striking departure from the many earlier examples of reclining nudes, starting at least as far back as the Renaissance with Giorgione's *Sleeping Venus*, all of which presented images of women as idealized in the artist's own Zone 1 imagination and projected out onto the canvas.

Figure 8.2a: Giorgione's (c 1510) Sleeping Venus

Figure 8.2b: Manet's 1863 Olympia

Such examples from science and art illustrate the essential point that not all eight zones have been a part of human experience from the beginning. In fact, most of them are fairly new additions. We have already seen, for instance, that even the basic division of human experience into inner and outer realms did not appear clearly in modern times before the 1641 publication of René Descartes' *Meditations on First Philosophy*, in which he divided the kosmos into an inner mind-stuff, *res cogitans*, and an "extended" world of material objects, *res extensa*. Almost immediately other philosophers such as John Locke took up the idea and it soon became common practice to think of reality in terms of entirely separate inner and outer dimensions.

Around the time of the Renaissance humankind was waking up to new perspectives, new forms of experience. Great changes occurred again near the end of the nineteenth century and during the early years of the twentieth century when a variety of new perspectives appeared in art, literature, philosophy, science, and religion. Gebser noticed these changes and identified them with the birth of a new "integral" consciousness, which we now understand as an advanced form of what Wilber terms *vision–logic*.[20]

It was during the year 1900, for instance, that Paul Cézanne, said to be "the first phenomenologist of art," labored to paint Mont Ste-Victoire exactly as it is experienced by the viewer (Zone 1). Similar efforts, though less exacting, had been underway since the 1860s by French impressionists such as Claude Monet, Pierre-Auguste Renoir, Berthe Morisot, and Edgar Degas.

By the 1920s surrealism became a significant movement in the visual arts, music, theater, and literature, expressing inner processes of thought and the mind. Perhaps best known among surrealist artists is Salvador Dali, while other notables included the Spanish painter Joan Miro and the German-French sculptor and poet Jean Arp. These artists were dealing with Zone 1 material, but framing it in free-form artistic styles that indicate a significant level of Zone 2 detachment.

Figure 8.3: Paul Cézanne's Mont Ste-Victoire, 1898

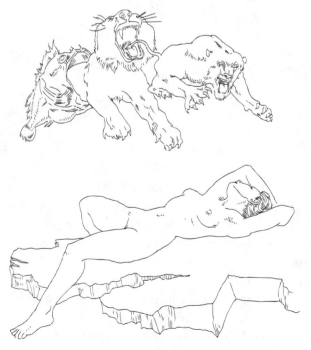

Figure 8.4: Salvador Dali - Dream Caused by the Flight of a Bee; 1944

In 1925, as we have seen, physicist Werner Heisenberg was writing the matrix equations to describe the inner properties of matter. This required a fully developed Zone 5 perspective and, because of the complexity of the interacting elements in these systems of mathematical operations, a mature Zone 7 understanding as well. Interestingly, the inner dimensions of the plural quadrants—Zones 3 and 7—were the last to find their way into full human awareness. Though Poincaré had anticipated these perspectives, it was not until well past midway through the twentieth century that systems theorists such as Karl Ludwig von Bertalanffy, Erich Jantsch, and Ervin Laszlo begin to examine the outer aspects of the lower right quadrant (Zone 8). At the same time Niklas Luhmann was breaking ground in the exploration of the inner self-organizing dynamics of networks of language and communication (Zone 7). Meanwhile, European structuralists and neo-structuralists explored the external aspects of language in terms of the shared knowledge and value systems represented in Zone 4.

Through all of this surprisingly little attention was given to the inner dimension of shared experience (Zone 3). The German-Jewish philosopher Martin Buber had written his celebrated essay, *Ich und Du* (*I and Thou*) all the way back in 1923, which examined the intersubjective depths experienced by persons sharing authentic relationships. His ideas were widely discussed in the U.S. during the 1960s, but more in terms of his emphasis on authenticity than his recognition of intersubjectivity.[21] At the time of the present writing there finally seems to be a growing interest in shared experience. For example, the Andrew Cohen community in Lenox, Massachusetts, has been developing a kind of shared consciousness effective in problem-solving situations, which they suspect may be the next major step in the evolution of human consciousness.

Certainly shared or collective consciousness is not new to human experience. Quakers have long referred to a "gathered meeting" as a powerful kind of unity awareness that occurs on rare occasions in their silent Sunday gatherings. I have experienced this myself. It is deeply rewarding and definitely something beyond a personal Zone 1 experience. However, it is difficult to collect information on this type of experience because it is not on the radar screen of our cultural awareness. I can only imagine that many primary cultures and contemplatives who practice together experience such group awareness on a regular basis. The latter may range from whirling dervishes to meditation and prayer circles.

One fascinating aspect of group consciousness is that it seems to express itself in both primitive and advanced forms. We might think of these as *pre-personal* and *post-personal* forms of collective experience. There is good reason to suspect that prior to the historical evolution of the mythic and mental structures of consciousness, especially during the ascendance of the magical structure of experience many thousands of years ago, group or tribal consciousness was the common and perhaps even the universal mode of experience. Later, with the evolution of the mythic and especially the mental structures, the experience of magical reality did not disappear but became submerged. As Freud discovered, it can reappear today in neurotic symptoms such as denial and obsessive-compulsive behavior. It can also reappear in a dark regressive form as occurred in twentieth century fascism. As Erich Fromm put it in the title of his book on the psychology of Germany during the Third Reich, it is an *Escape from Freedom*; it is, an escape from individuality and the choices and responsibilities that go with it. In its most ancient form, however, it is likely that it was much more healthy, normal, and innocent.

Modern communities working toward collective intelligence seem to be going in quite a different direction. The Andrew Cohen community, for example, appears to be finding its way toward a kind of shared intelligence that preserves personal consciousness as an active feature of one's total experience. Hence this group consciousness seems post-personal rather than pre-personal.[22]

It is possible that members of primary cultures in the modern world have come this route as well. Developmental theorists such as Wilber are sometimes faulted for placing traditional cultures into low developmental categories. Actually, Wilber has written virtually nothing about primary societies in the modern world, but a few theorists have no doubt been guilty of this. Clare Graves, for instance, whose developmental theory of personal value structures, rooted in 1950s and 1960s research and forming the foundation for modern Spiral Dynamics, certainly viewed primary cultures as developmentally backward.[23] But, as every psychologist knows, it is very difficult to produce tests of developmental maturity, intelligence, or personality that are cross-culturally valid. A good guess is that certain seemingly magical cultures of the modern world, such as South American tribal societies and Australian Aborigines, have actually managed to make it into the twenty-first century without losing touch with the magical and mythic dimensions of their experience, of which European culture after The Enlightenment became seriously deprived. In Gebser's sense of *integral*, that is, living all the structures of consciousness, this would make them more integral than the average resident of modern New York City.

Horizontal Evolution and Vertical Development

We now turn to the relationship between horizontal evolution and vertical development. Here I am especially interested in the extent to which the historical appearance of new perspectives might have been the fruit of the vertical growth of new cognitive structures. In this it is well to keep in mind that even some of the lower stages of development, such as Piaget's concrete operations, which we examined in Chapter 4, can produce surprisingly high levels of intellectual achievement. These must occur, however, within the logical framework of each stage. This is a point that is sometimes missed by critics of the developmental view. Simply showing that a person or a society has accomplished something remarkable—for instance, navigating primitive boats over hundreds of miles of open sea—does not in itself prove that its people are developmentally advanced. It just means that they have made good use of the intellectual resources they have at hand. It is the nature of what is done that tells us from which developmental stage it came.

With this in mind let us again recall Descartes' seventeenth century "discovery" of the distinction between inner and outer realms of experience. This discovery required a highly-refined level of abstract thinking just as his invention of analytic geometry that gave birth to the whole notion of three dimensional or "Cartesian" space. Newton relied on the latter concept of space to craft his amazingly powerful mathematics of celestial motion. Both of these men were reasoning at least at Piaget's formal operations level (Wilber's *formop*), but it is not clear that they required more than this. On the other hand, Heisenberg's matrix algebra calls for the more advanced structure of systems thinking found in *vision–logic*. Likewise, Niklas Luhmann's concept of the self-organizing interior of linguistic networks, David Bohm's and Ervin Laszlo's deep holographic visions of the cosmos, and Karl Pribram's holonomic theory of the brain, all demand this advanced form of thinking.

From the above examples we might suspect that formal operations thinking, at least where science is concerned, is largely constrained to Zone 6, whereas the next developmental stage, or vision logic, opens out into Zone 5 and perhaps also into Zones 7 and 8 as well. Thus, it would appear that as the forms of thinking that undergird mathematics and science become more complex, the number of perspectives available to scientists and mathematicians increases as well.

The situation is less clear when it comes to the arts, but one theme that seems apparent is that starting around the turn of the twentieth century the ability of artists to intentionally shift between perspectives increased dramatically. Realism, as seen in Manet's *Olympia*, in Figure 8.2b earlier, required a consciously fixed view from Zone 6, the external perception of an external objective world, so as not to contaminate the work with elements of fantasy and imagination. Cézanne's turn-of-the-century painting of Mont Sainte-Victoire in Figure 8.3 was an intentional effort to depict the mountain straight from the perspective of Zone 1, the inner dimension of experience itself. As noted above, impressionism was seeking the same view. Soon a variety of expressionist schools such as surrealism and symbolist art were digging into the depths of Zone 1.

Pablo Picasso was remarkable for his fluent ability to represent multiple perspectives of the same physical object while working these into abstract aesthetic forms. Clearly this required a kind of vision-logic of the eye, and indeed it is not surprising that Gebser considered his works, such as *Guernica*,[24] to represent integral consciousness as he then understood it.

Figure 8.5: Guernica – Picasso, 1937

Contemporary art takes too many forms to explore in detail here, but certain artists such as Mark Tansey seem to have a gift for exploiting multiple frames of reference. His 1981 work, *The Innocent Eye*, for instance, depicts a cow viewing a painting of two other cows apparently relaxing by a tree, one standing and the other laying down while looking out of the painting at the "real" cow. Nearby several middle-aged men in black suits look on, and someone in a lab coat is taking notes. This all appears to take place in an art gallery with one of Monet's paintings of a hay stack along the wall in the background. It is difficult to count the number of inner and outer perspectives hinted at in this work, but one thing for sure is that the artist intended for us to be aware of them.

Figure 8.6: Mark Tansey - The Innocent Eye, 1981

Considering art created during the past two or three decades, there is an increasing tendency for at least certain works of visual art, theater, literature, and music to invite us into an artistic moment in which we become aware of actually being conscious in the art experience. Perhaps this is the meaning of Tansey's *The Innocent Eye*. For my part, minimalist works such as Mark Rothko's nearly empty canvases seem to invite us to be aware of ourselves in the act of standing before them. Giving these works titles such as *#20* discourages the viewer from trying to read them as representational or even abstract objects and encourages us simply to experience the moment in their presence. Likewise, the productions of the German performance artist and shaman Joseph Beuys seem to invite us into self-reflection rather than toward interpretations of his creations. For his 1974 performance piece, *I Like America and America Likes Me*, he arrived at the John F. Kennedy Airport wrapped in felt and was carried by ambulance to an art museum where he spent a week in a large cage with a live coyote. This performance had something to do with his love for animals, but no attempt to put a simple or even complex interpretation on it seems successful. Basically, the event, which you can now see as a streaming video, seems to invite us into an altered sense of ourselves in relationship to the coyote and the artist hidden in his felt blanket.

Figure 8.7: I Like America and America Likes Me – Joseph Beuys

The thread of conscious experience as an intentional aspect of art can be traced in numerous contemporary art shows, books, and performance works dedicated to just this topic. What is remarkable about all this is the fluid perspective explicit or implicit in many forms of modern art. From the contemplative sounds of Pauline Oliveros' *Deep Listening* to art exhibits such as the University of Kentucky Art Museum's glass and pottery show, *Opening the Gates of Consciousness*, to San Francisco's

1999 CCAC Institute exhibit, *Searchlight: Consciousness at the Millennium*, each actively exploring "conscious art" that encourages the viewer to be aware of his or her own experience in the presence of these works, one cannot help but be impressed at the ease with which contemporary artists such as Tansey play with experiential perspectives the way Picasso played with spatial ones. Consistent with this line of thinking, the contemporary Danish artist Olafur Eliasson describes his art's ultimate goal as creating a state of self-awareness and reflection that encourages us to "See yourself seeing yourself."

Figure 8.8: The Weather Project – Olafur Eliasson, 2003.
(Photographer: Jens Ziehe)

Though much is yet to be learned of the details, the above seems to suggest that the emergence of these perspectives is intimately tied to the developmental level of those persons who experience them. And, it would seem that the turn of the twenty-first century, like the turn of the twentieth century before it, has brought fundamental shifts in the way the world is understood. These shifts exhibit themselves not only in the large-scale emergence of more refined developmental structures of consciousness, but also in a growing awareness of the many inflections of experience articulated in Wilber's eight perspectives. As these become increasingly familiar and as they are mastered the way the basic inner and outer dimensions of experience were mastered after Descartes first mapped them, we see the appearance of a new form of integral consciousness, a horizontal articulation and integration of perspectives unimagined even a few decades ago. In this way, emerging twenty-first century consciousness embraces a nimbleness that allows it access to aspects of the Kosmos unimagined by our ancestors.

9. The Many Faces of Integral Consciousness

The future of the Earth depends on a change of consciousness ... and the change is bound to come. But it is left to [humans] to decide if they will collaborate for this change or it will have to be enforced upon them by the power of crashing circumstances.

The Mother

All the evolution we know of proceeds from the vague to the definite.

Charles Sanders Peirce

A Short History of Integral Consciousness

The word *integral* has become fashionable during the early years of the twenty-first century replacing the more linear sounding *holism* popular in the 1980s and 1990s. Both words reflect a growing appreciation of the fact that nearly anything you can think of—from foods to ecologies, and from economies to people—represents a manifold of interpenetrating facets, not one of which can realistically be teased out, studied, or manipulated separately from the others. Another way of approaching this simple truth is to realize that every aspect of human reality as well as the world of nature can be seen and experienced from many different perspectives, a point made over and over again in the previous chapters. With these thoughts in mind let me take a moment to introduce several leading figures in the history of a concept—the idea of integral consciousness.

Sri Aurobindo, the Mother, and Integral Yoga

Sri Aurobindo first introduced the notion of an integral approach to consciousness and spirituality during the early decades of the twentieth century. As we saw in the preceding chapter, the integral yoga he developed with his partner, The Mother, was designed to unite body, mind, and spirit in a single spiritually transformed being. This was an important move away from traditional schools of yoga that tended to foster an identification with the subtle and nonphysical aspects of human experience while turning away from the material world and the physical body. This yoga was also integral in another less celebrated but perhaps even more important way. It could be practiced in the midst of an active life in the world. Sri Aurobindo did much of his own early spiritual work while actively managing a newspaper. During this period he meditated while walking back and forth through his apartments.

At its most advanced level integral yoga becomes "supramental yoga," which strives to bring the divine energies of the kosmos down into the physical body, transforming it on all levels. The ideal of a complete metamorphosis of the mind and body into a pure spiritual substance is not unique to integral yoga. It is found in one form or another in spiritual traditions such as the Tibetan Dzogchen and Buddhist notions of the rainbow body of light, and in the Taoist idea of the perfected Immortals. Something like it was also said to be seen in the transubstantiation of Christ. What is so unique about integral yoga is that this change is sought through practices carried out while living a more or less ordinary life in the world, rather than by withdrawing into an all-consuming monastic practice. The transformation moves down into the physical body itself, changing it right down to its atoms.

Jean Gebser's Integral Consciousness

The first major theorist to actually use the phrase "integral consciousness" seems to have been the German poet and cultural philosopher Jean Gebser. We are already familiar with his five major structures of consciousness, each associated with its own worldview. Briefly, the first or *archaic* structure represents a transitional consciousness from pre-human hominids to the earliest human beings. Gebser did not claim to know very much about this form of experience, noting only that it was metaphorically like sleep. He often cited the words of the Taoist philosopher Chuang-tzu, "Dreamlessly the true men of earlier times slept." The second is the *magical* structure of consciousness, associated with an ancient prepersonal worldview in which magical thinking and magical causation served in place of today's logical thinking and scientific causation. Next, though extending well back into the magical period, came the rise of the *mythic* structure and its worldview of powerful and majestic gods and goddesses. These great beings are still remembered today in mythologies from all around the world. The *mental* structure of consciousness emerged during the first millennia before Christ, becoming apparent with the earliest Greek philosophers such as Parmenides, Pythagoras, Thales, and Heraclitus, who turned to reason and logic for explanations of fundamental questions about reality.

While the mental structure of consciousness seems to have been virtually lost during the Middle Ages, it returned at the beginning of the Renaissance expanding to incorporate the dramatic new feature of perspectival awareness that powered the efflorescence of Renaissance art and architecture. It also inspired an explosion of interest in geography and global exploration as well as making possible an entirely new form of mathematics in Descartes' three-dimensional analytic geometry.

Each of Gebser's structures of consciousness has its own positive and negative features. For instance, on the positive side the magical structure is associated with music, with its mysterious power to transport us out of the here and now and into imagined landscapes and forgotten times and places. Falling in love is also magical. When we are in love we feel as if we share the same inner space and even the same sense of being as the beloved. The mythic structure of consciousness, on the other hand, is associated with poetry and the grand epics of the gods, goddesses, and of the creation of the world. In spiritual and religious contexts these mythic stories lend purpose and meaning to our individual lives. Without them we must seek life's meaning though reason alone, or slide back into a purely magical understanding of life's mysteries. But while the mental structure is an excellent tool for coping with the demands of a harsh material world, its efforts to create meaning, for example through existential philosophy and rational theology, seem bleak and barren compared to the richness of the stories told of the lives of the Buddha, Lao Tzu, Muhammad, and Christ.

Beyond these structures of consciousness, Gebser found evidence for the emergence of a new *integral* structure coming onto the scene around the beginning of the twentieth century. As we saw in the previous chapter, this was a period of a remarkable multiplication of the perspectives from and through which the world could be experienced. It was as if artists, poets, scientists, mathematicians, and others were suddenly becoming aware of new ways to approach human experience, ways we can understand in terms of Wilber's eight zones or perspectives. This new plasticity was one of the hallmarks of the integral experience that Gebser identified. Another hallmark was a "diaphanous" quality to appearances, such that the world is suffused paradoxically with a divine inner illumination while at the same time becoming increasingly clear and solid. This experience, surprisingly suggestive of causal realm perception, is what leads many people who have studied Gebser's writings or who knew him personally to believe that late in his life he had become familiar with advanced states of consciousness. In line with this, the widely respected Zen scholar, D.T. Suzuki, personally verified to Gebser that he had experienced at least one extended episode of Kenshō,[1] which Gebser identified as integral consciousness.

Perhaps Gebser's most valuable contribution was the insight that integral consciousness implies a harmonious integration of all the structures of consciousness. This idea, at the very core of Gebser's notion of what it means to be integral, turns out to be profound. Let us take a moment to explore it. Along the way I will add some ideas of my own, suggested by years studying the nature of consciousness experience and the mind.

Gebser's insight unpacked

An important idea here is that structures of consciousness, like many other complex structures such as living organisms, tend to form themselves into hierarchies.[2] What is more, these hierarchies mature according to developmental rules. In the case of structures of consciousness such hierarchical development can be seen in the mental and experiential growth of the individual as well as in the long developmental history of civilization. As we have seen, during the early years of the twentieth century James Baldwin was one of the first psychologists to map out the developmental process as it unfolds from childhood up through advanced levels of adult maturation. We have also seen that Piaget as well as many recent cognitive psychologists tracked attendant changes in mental growth. Gebser, on the other hand, was the first modern scholar to follow the unfolding of these same structures of consciousness through history, noting the cultural transformations that accompanied them.[3] And he was the first scholar to introduce the idea of "structures" of consciousness. Now let's explore these notions in terms of hierarchies.

For a clearer picture of how these hierarchies might play out at the personal level let's look at an example of a child in the process of growing from predominantly magical thinking into the stage of mythical thinking—in Piaget's terms from the preoperational stage to the concrete operations stage. For most children this would occur somewhere between five and seven years of age. Magical thinking, however, does not actually disappear. It is still healthy and well during play activities where it reappears under the guidance of the newer and now dominant mythic structure. Dolls, teddy bears, and cloth animals, as well as toy cars, boats, and trucks, all retain magical—read imaginary— qualities, but now find themselves under the influence of a more mature kind of thought process. Interestingly, at night and with the approach of sleep the magical structure can rebound in full career, bringing with it the prospect of a visit from the monster in the closet or the awful folks living under the bed or in the cellar. Only later in adolescence or even adulthood do these sorts of apparitions come under more or less complete control as the mental structure finally matures. But even then the ability to open ourselves to magical experiences in music, art, love, and poetry, are not lost, and can return under the gentle stewardship of a rational adult ego.

Likewise, as the mind matures the spiritual and religious inspirations of the mythic structure of consciousness, with its compelling values such as *truth*, *beauty*, and *compassion*, are not lost when rational thought replaces the mythic imagination as the dominant way of thinking. Rather, in the healthy personality these are balanced by the faculty of reason. It was exactly in this spirit that Carl Jung stressed the value of a mature ego in regulating the powerful archetypal (read mythical) forces of the collective unconsciousness. The same message can be found in the writings of contemporary depth psychologist James Hillman. Both emphasize the importance of a strong and mature ego for keeping one's feet planted firmly on the solid ground. But both also stress the role of the archetypal or mythic unconscious as a source of life and vitality in the psyche, and as the wellspring of a palpable sense of life's destiny. We see in all this the importance of living into our magic and mythic experiences, but cultivating them as servants to the mental structure and ultimately to the higher structures of consciousness that unfold, as Sri Aurobindo would have said, in the further evolution of consciousness. Or in Wilber's terms, with the developmental and evolutionary unfolding of higher structures of cognitive and spiritual growth.

The chief point to be taken from the above is that in a healthy personality the magic and mythic structures of consciousness, which first emerged in childhood as *preconventional* structures, are later put into the service of the *conventional* mind governed by an adult ego, and later may even become servants to more advanced *postconventional* structures such as Sri Aurobindo's illumined or intuitive minds. This basic pattern applies to the historical evolution of structures of consciousness as well as to the mental growth of the individual person. For instance, Paleolithic shamans probably operated in terms of what we would today call preconventional magical thinking,[4] but contemporary shamans, especially those living in the modern world, are likely to be regulating their magical technologies with conventional mental or even higher structures.[5]

Expanding on these ideas we might suspect that a general principle is to be found here. It is that each newly emerging structure of consciousness becomes the governing form of experience while older structures can either become respected servants of the new structure, as is the case in the healthy personality, or the new structure can attempt to suppress the older structures and rule in isolation. In the latter case the older structures become unconscious or shadow presences that continue to act outside of awareness like unruly children. Depth psychologists such as Carl Jung and James Hillman have written volumes on this topic. What is more, it seems that in the absence of a well-developed ego, virtually any structure of consciousness can practically hijack the personality resulting in religious fanaticism (magic or mythic), fascist political ideologies (mythic), as well as disturbed and disturbing interpersonal behavior. The story of structures gone wrong is complex and worth a few volumes in and of itself. The point here is that a healthy personality is governed from the top, that is, the highest structure that has yet emerged, while the earlier structures remain onboard enriching the texture of life's experience.

The Many Faces of Integral Consciousness

With the above reflections in mind let's back up and consider just what integral consciousness might mean to us today. In fact we will find that the idea of integral consciousness can mean a number of things, each correct in its own way. I list some of the important ones below.

Integral Consciousness as Highest Level or Ordinary Mind

As we saw in chapter 7, Wilber has often referred to a specific developmental structure of mind as "integral." This is the level of *vision–logic*, corresponding to Sri Aurobindo's *higher mind*.[6]

More specifically, it is the highest level of systems thinking before one begins to experience Sri Aurobindo's *illumined mind*, thus entering the transpersonal realm of experience. The individual at this level sees the world in terms of systems of interconnecting processes as well as understanding things in terms of systems of interconnecting ideas. He or she understands that these systems can be viewed from different perspectives and in different lights, thus the view is pluralistic. It is also integral, however, in that whole interlocking systems of understanding can be embraced in a single vision. A scientist with vision-logic, for instance, might see both astronomy and physics overlapping in a common set of mathematical principles. Thus, great theorists such as Albert Einstein and Steven Hawking could set forth mathematically-based models of the cosmos that span from the subatomic phenomena to the nature of gravity and the creation of the universe in the big bang. Modern understandings of the relationships between economics, ecology, and global weather require this perspective as well, if we are to be effective in future planning around the many important issues that involve the entire planet.

Integral Consciousness as the Integration of Altitude

As we saw above, Gebser's idea of integral consciousness was to live all the structures all the time. This means a condition of experience in which all of the structures of consciousness co-exist in harmony. Since we have already examined this view in some detail, let us pass on to other notions of integral consciousness.

Integral Consciousness as the Integration of Primal Perspectives

In chapter 8 we explored the horizontal evolution of consciousness. The main idea in that chapter was that new primal perspectives on the Kosmos seem to have accompanied the historical appearance of new vertical structures of consciousness.

Wilber's articulation of the eight primal perspectives, two in each quadrant and four in each side of the AQAL square, gave us a useful roadmap for developing this notion. But since this idea has already been examined, let us again move on.

Integral Consciousness as the Harmony of Body, Mind, and Spirit

It is common practice these days to apply the term "integral" to any idea or practice that attempts to harmonize body, mind, and spirit. Of course, these also represent three levels of reality— the physical world, the world of thought and experience, and the world of the spirit. The latter may mean different things to different people, ranging from conventional religious notions to mystical inspirations. In any case, this is a kind of generic brand application of the term integral to give a more unified idea of the way things work. There is nothing wrong with this, but it is worth keeping in mind that when you see the word "integral" in reference to anything from whole foods to various forms of spiritual practices it does not mean that Sri Aurobindo or The Mother, or Ken Wilber, have any connection with it. It is for this reason that Wilber has adopted the acronym AQAL to identify his own integral philosophy and set it apart from the many other forms of integral philosophy and practice.

Integral Consciousness and the Prime Directive

Many of the ideas above can be united under the roof of Wilber's *Prime Directive*, which is to optimize all quadrants at all levels.[7] In other words, the point is to seek conditions that promote optimal life across each of the four quadrants, and to do so for every individual, or every being, at each developmental level. Now let us see what this idea means in terms of conscious experience.

To begin with, it suggests that we can speak most meaningfully about integral consciousness only when all of our developmental structures are functioning in harmony. This was Gebser's idea of integral consciousness, and here we refer to it as the *vertical integration* of structures at all levels or altitudes. In the preceding pages we saw that a healthy personality relies on all such structures working together harmoniously while governed from the highest structure the individual has yet fully developed. It also suggests the *horizontal integration* of consciousness across the four quadrants and even the eight perspectives, each representing a different dimension of experience. As we have seen, the historical flowering of new vertical structures of consciousness brought with it the blossoming of new horizontal perspectives as well. These include the intersubjectivity of the lower left quadrant as well as inner aspects of both right-hand quadrants.

Should we then gauge "integral consciousness" on a scale that reckons the ease with which a person switches from zone to zone through this network of experiential perspectives? Or the extent to which a person might hold multiple perspectives at once? Conscious experience is indeed nimble, especially as we master the more advanced developmental structures. And along the way it becomes ever more possible for us to experience the world, including ourselves, through an increasing number of lenses, or perspectives. Yet even with all these considerations in the balance, it would seem that if the idea of "integral consciousness" is remarkable or special it should mean something more than a benchmark summary of the vertical and horizontal reach of an individual's experience. In other words, we would like integral consciousness to mean something more profound than something obtained through a laundry list of characteristics. So let us move on.

Integral Consciousness as Enlightenment

Might we say that "integral consciousness" means enlightenment? In other words, could integral consciousness be yet another way of talking about enlightenment? The notion is indeed appealing on first nod. But unfortunately the word "enlightenment" has about as many meanings as the word "integral." Briefly, the word *enlightenment* became a regular part of spiritual conversation in the U.S. and Europe during the 1960s and 1970s when Western civilization found itself seriously interested in the spiritual traditions of the East for the first time since the 1890s and the turn of the twentieth century.[8] Initially much of this interest came from California, at first through figures such as Aldous Huxley, the prominent author and cultural icon who became fascinated with the Indian philosophy of Vedanta, and Alan Watts whose many books on Zen almost single-handedly popularized Buddhism in the West. Another important figure of the period was Michael Murphy who co-founded Esalen Institute, soon to become and remain the foremost center for the exploration of human potentials in the world. Others such as the enormously popular Ram Dass continued to spread interest in Eastern spiritual traditions and their notions of enlightenment. All this transpired during the same period in which powerful mind-altering drugs such as LSD and mescaline came into wide use, bringing home the reality of states of consciousness beyond the ordinary.

The problem, however, is that the word "enlightment" does not have a single meaning. For example, some people think of it as a state of consciousness that contains all knowledge, or believe that it offers complete freedom from worry and pain. Others view it as a high spiritual condition in which one's essence ascends to the divine.

Turning to Eastern sacred texts for a clear definition of enlightenment is not very helpful. To begin with, "enlightenment" is an English word with no unequivocal counterpart in Eastern languages. Its modern usage in the West harkens back to the eighteenth century *Age of Enlightenment* and the latter's emphasis on rationality and reason as the basis of knowledge and authority. Nowadays the word is used as a kind of do-all translation of many terms in Eastern spiritual texts that represent advanced or ultimate states of spiritual realization.[9] On closer examination these signify a variety of different metaphors such as realization, awakening, liberation, release from the wheel of birth and death, and so on.

Wilber has given more than one definition of enlightenment as his own thinking on the topic evolved over the years. In *Integral Spirituality* he states:

> Enlightenment is the realization of oneness with all the major states and major structures that are in existence at any given time in history.[10]

As Wilber himself points out, the most shocking thing about this definition is that it changes with time. In other words, as human consciousness evolves, so does enlightenment! It is apparent that this definition sounds very much like the idea of integral consciousness we examined earlier while considering the Prime Directive. It does not explicitly include the horizontal dimension of consciousness, but comes very close to doing so in its emphasis on developmental structures which, as we have seen, give birth to multiple perspectives and the horizontal articulation of consciousness. The idea that an adequate definition of enlightenment includes all such structures also agrees with the notion that integral consciousness must include an integration of altitude, or all major structures of consciousness, in other words, Gebser's worldviews.

Wilber's definition importantly includes *states* of consciousness as well as structures. The ability to inhabit states of consciousness beyond the ordinary, especially ones associated with subtle, causal, and even nondual awareness, is central to many views of enlightenment. Thus, we might think someone living, for example, in a nondual state is "enlightened," though that person may possess only modest cognitive or moral maturity. I invite the reader to consider this possibility when reflecting on the careers of some of the "enlightened masters" who have visited the U.S. and Europe during the past 40 years or so.

In any case, this is a perfectly good definition of enlightenment, and we can also take it for a good description of integral consciousness in its grandest sense. One could hardly argue that someone who meets these criteria is not enlightened. On the other hand it is certainly not the simple but powerful notion of enlightenment many people seek.

Integral Consciousness and Enlightenment: A Summing Up

This all brings us to an important conclusion. No single combination of states and structures can represent perfect enlightenment valid in all times and all places. Perhaps this should be no surprise when we reflect on the fact that we live in a world of constant evolutionary change. Let us note, however, that this view does not detract from the great spiritual vanguards of the present and past. Their personal and social accomplishments stand even higher when we realize that they, like us, lived and labored in a world of hardship and transformation—a constantly changing landscape in which all personal and social constants are subject to evolutionary growth, transformation, and increasing complexity. It is this evolutionary process that has given us the richness of our own amazingly creative and intelligent nature as well as the abundance of the flowering natural world around us. We all have in us a yearning for a perfect and ideal state which, once realized, would mean the end to strife and a termination of the urge toward further change. But on deeper reflection we may realize such a state would ultimately lead to boredom and stagnation.

All these conclusions lead us to a place halfway between the perennialists on the one hand and the postmodernists on the other. In 1945 when Aldous Huxley published his groundbreaking book, *The Perennial Philosophy*, he set in motion a stream of scholarship that emphasized the universality of spiritual growth in all major wisdom traditions. As time went by other names were added to this tradition such as Huston Smith, Joseph Campbell, Michael Washburn, and Ken Wilber's own early works. By the final decades of the late twentieth century, however, a new generation of academic religious scholars strongly influenced by European postmodernism launched an all-out attack on the perennialists, emphasizing the relativistic preeminence of culture, language, and history in any "religious" experience, and debunking the idea that common threads lie at their core.[11] At the time of this writing we are experiencing a return of the perennialist view, but in a more sophisticated form. Wilber's entire work on the importance of perspectives as undergirding human experience can be thought of in this light.

Our observations here, stressing the importance of the evolutionary moment in any complete understanding of enlightenment or integral consciousness, are a step in this direction. They recognize the importance of the changing evolutionary moment in any conversation about such topics. On the other hand, here as well as in Wilber's work we are seeking the universal dimensions of consciousness that mark us as human beings. In this sense Wilber and I are both twenty-first century perennialists. And, if you agree with us, so are you.[12]

And there was the ultimate paradox and the final mystery. Life moves ever outwards into infinite possibilities, and yet all things are perfect and finished in every single moment, their end attained.

—David Zindell [13]

Endnotes

Introduction

1. D. Zindell. (1998). *War in Heaven; Book Three of a Requiem for Homo Sapiens*. London: HarperCollins, p. 734.

2. It is worth noting that the philosophical school of phenomenology has been faithful to the study of consciousness since its beginnings in the writings of Edmund Husserl and Martin Heidegger, but employing such abstruse language and restrained formats that for the most part only other phenomenologists can read it.

Chapter 1

1. From the often quoted statement by psychologist George Miller: "'Consciousness' is a word worn smooth by a million tongues. Depending upon the figure of speech chosen it is a state of being, a substance, a process, a place, an epiphenomenon, an emergent aspect of matter, or the only true reality." George Miller, (1962). *Psychology: The Science of Mental Life*. New York: Harper & Row.

2. J. Jaynes. (1976). *The Origin of Consciousness in the Breakdown of the Bicameral Mind*. Boston: Houghton Mifflin, p. 2.

3. At least this is the common consensus. There actually is some question as to whether Descartes might have been using the term in its older sense. See: Angefertigt von Boris Hennig; retrieved June 1, 2007, from http://www.borishennig.de/texte/descartes/diss/. [von Boris Hennig (1974). *Was bedeutet 'conscientia' bei Descartes?* Der Fakultät für Sozialwissenschalften und Philosopie der Universität Leipzig. Dissertation.]

4. A *simple idea* is something like the color red or the taste of salt, while *complex ideas* were said to be compounded of simple ideas, for example the idea of an apple or a writing desk.

5. This idea was taken to heart by scientists throughout the world, and formed the rational basis for the investigation of nature though observation.

6. John Locke. (1689). *An Essay Concerning Human Understanding*. (IV, iv, 2).

7.   All this is drawn from fairly recent Western history. *Cit*, the Indian Sanskrit term most like the western word *consciousness* is much older, with a long and complex history of its own. To address its history would take a book in itself, but for those interested, Bina Gupta's (2003) *Cit consciousness*, from Oxford University Press, offers an excellent history and analysis. Terms similar to the English word *consciousness* are found in Tibetan, Chinese, and Japanese writings as well. The etymologies of these words are complex, as you might imagine, partly because they are influenced by the Sanskrit *cit* and the English *consciousness*.

8.   William James. (1912/1996). *Essays in Radical Empiricism*. Lincoln, NB: University of Nebraska Press, p. 3.

9.   Ibid.

10.   This is certainly not to say that it is not useful to have terms such as *waterfalls* or *storms*, or even that they do exhibit unique dynamics that define them as physical systems. It is just that when all is said and done they are, at bottom, water flowing, and wind and rain, each acting in a particular way.

11.   In this sense the "laws of physics" started out as the laws of God, on the same plane as the moral edicts of the church. Now they are understood simply as regularities, and there is even discussion as to whether they are the same throughout the cosmos.

12.   Gravity seemed to imply action or causation at a distance, an idea entirely contrary to the reductionistic notions of causation espoused by Descartes and subscribed to by Newton.

13.   I will not attempt to review the contortions that Locke and other philosophers were forced through in order to get from this view to a convincing justification for the objective empirical science we are all familiar with today.

14.   Carolyn Wells (Ed.). *A Nonsense Anthology*. NY: Scribner's, 1902.

Chapter 2

1.   William James. (1890/1981). *The Principles of Psychology*. Cambridge, MA: Harvard University Press, p. 233.

2.   Ibid., p. 140.

3.   Ibid., p. 139.

4.   See Ralph Pret. (2005). *Onflow: Dynamics of consciousness and experience.* Cambridge, MA: MIT Press.

5.   Alfred North Whitehead. (1929/1978). *Process and reality: An essay in cosmology.* New York: Collier Macmillan; p.68. Referring to James (1911/1996). *Some problems of philosophy.* Lincoln, NB: University of Nebraska Press; p.155.

Chapter 3

1.   G. Spencer-Brown. (1979). *Laws of Form.* New York: E. P. Dutton, p. xxix.

2.   Retrieved June 1, 2007, from http://www.thefreedictionary.com/four-part+harmony.

3.   The bubonic plague.

4.   Here I refer to our work on the nature of consciousness and its implications. Wilber's overall philosophy is impressive in scope and in many areas transcends my own knowledge and interests.

5.   Interestingly the idea of "the myth of the given" was originally proposed by an American philosopher named Wilfrid Sellars in a paper presented in the University of London Special Lectures on Philosophy for 1955-56, delivered on March 1, 8, and 15, 1956, under the title "The Myth of the Given: Three Lectures on Empiricism and the Philosophy of Mind."

6.   The full title was, *Meditations on the First Philosophy: In Which the Existence of God and the Distinction Between Mind and Body are Demonstrated.* (The original title also made reference to a proof of the existence of the soul, but after one critic observed that the word "soul" appears nowhere in the text Descartes changed it to its present form.)

7.   About which John Knox, an early twentieth century author and wit wrote the now famous lines:

There was a young man who said "God
Must think it exceedingly odd
If he finds that this tree
Continues to be
When there's no one about in the Quad."

"Dear Sir, your astonishment's odd;
I am always about in the Quad,
And that's why the tree
Will continue to be
Since observed by Yours faithfully, God."

8.   G. Spencer-Brown. (1979). *Laws of form*. New York: E. P. Dutton.

9.   In an interview for the *Shambhala Sun* magazine, Wilber explained his use of the term *Kosmos*: "Kosmos" is an old Pythagorean term, which means the entire universe in all its many dimensions: physical, emotional, mental and spiritual. Retrieved June 1, 2007, from http://www.shambhalasun.com/index.php?option=com_content&task=view&id=2059&Itemid=244.

10.   E.g., see Peter Atkins. (2004). *Galileo's Finger: The Ten Great Ideas of Science*. NYC: Oxford University Press.

11.   Reproduced with the permission of Ken Wilber.

12.   We will return to this point in chapter 8 where we examine the historical evolution of the quadrant perspectives.

13.   From Lewis Carroll. (1865). *Alice's Adventures in Wonderland*. Retrieved June 1, 2007, from http://www.literature.org/authors/carroll-lewis/alices-adventures-in-wonderland/.

Chapter 4

1.   James Mark Baldwin. (1930). *History of Psychology in Autobiography*. Worcester, MA: Clark University Press. Retrieved on June 1, 2007, from http://psychclassics.yorku.ca/Baldwin/murchison.htm.

2.   A similar story is told in *The Republic*, Book X, where Plato recounts the *Myth of Er*. In it souls are led to the Plain of Forgetfulness where they drink from the River of Forgetfulness whose waters no vessel can hold, causing them to forget their heavenly origins before being swept "like meteors" to their births. The idea that infants are born, in William Wordsworth's words "trailing clouds of glory," was popular among 19th century Transcendentalists such as Ralph Waldo Emerson and Henry David Thoreau.

3.   M. Gazzanniga. (2005). *The Ethical Brain*. Washington, DC: Dana Press.

4. Retrieved August 10, 2007, from http://answers.yahoo.com/question/ index?qid=20070805110036AAmjY9h and http://www.exploratorium. edu/memory/earlymemory/memoryform.html.

5. Or, "Old wine in new skins."

6. Ken Wilber. (2000b). *Integral Psychology*. Boston: Shambhala, pp. 132–33.

7. In fact, infants are born with a kind of elemental grasping reflex that allows them to immediately cling to their mothers, but they lose it within a few weeks and do not reacquire it as a learned behavior until about the third month after birth.

8. W. James. (1890/1981). *The Principles of Psychology*. Cambridge, MA: Harvard University Press, p. 462.

9. Ken Wilber. (1980). *The Atman Project*. Wheaton, IL: Theosophical Publishing House, p. 8.

10. Most of this description of the development of the sense of self in the infant is based on the writings of M.S. Mahler., F. Pine and A. Bergman, (1975). *The psychological birth of the human infant*. New York: Basic Books. Also, M. S. Mahler. (1979). *Separation–individuation: The selected papers of Margret S. Mahler Vol. II*. New York: Jason Aronson.

11. Though most phenomenologists argue that to be conscious involves some degree of self-awareness in the "weak sense" that experience must contain a self-affiliation or some degree of *mineness*.

12. For example, see Singer and Revenson's (1998) *A Piaget Primer: How a Child Thinks* for an excellent review of Piaget's basic theory.

13. Richard Hughes. (1928). *A High Wind in Jamaica: The Innocent Voyage*. New York: New American Library, p. 99.

Chapter 5

1. James Mark Baldwin, (1930). *History of Psychology in Autobiography*. Worcester, MA: Clark University Press, p. 22. Retrieved June 1, 2007 from http://psychclassics.yorku.ca/Baldwin/murchison.htm.

2. The phrase *integral psychology* is found in a number of scholarly traditions, including the writings by and about Sri Aurobindo, but here it is used specifically to refer to the psychology that flows from the AQAL model of Ken Wilber (1995).

3.   Actually Piaget understood that different kinds of tasks are often mastered at different developmental rates, referring to this as horizontal *decalage*, but he did not emphasize this concept greatly and it was all but forgotten by his successors.

4.   Terry Winograd. (1972). *Understanding Natural Language*. New York: Academic Press.

5.   Reproduced with the permission of Ken Wilber.

6.   Reproduced with the permission of Ken Wilber.

7.   Ken Wilber, Jack Engler and Daniel P. Brown. (1986). *Transformations of consciousness: Conventional and Contemplative Perspectives on Development*. Boston: New Science Library, p. 67. (Part 1: The Spectrum of Consciousness).

8.   As John B. Watson observed in the early days of behavioral psychology, infants begin life with an undifferentiated sense of pleasure and pain that, over the years, becomes articulated into an increasing number of emotions. Only in adolescence, for example, can most people begin to experience such subtle and complex emotions as nostalgia.

9.   For more details about these developmental stages see, e.g., Robert Kegan (1995), and Ken Wilber (1983, 2000).

10.   J. Broughton. (1987). *Critical Theories of Psychological Development*. New York: Springer.

11.   This was not actually her real name, which is long since forgotten.

12.   Modern youth seem to mature more quickly both physically and intellectually than their parents and grandparents. There is probably a host of factors involved, but at least one of them is certainly the overwhelming complexity of the postmodern environment.

13.   J. Loevinger. (1976). *Ego Development*. San Francisco: Jossey-Bass.

14.   Loevinger felt that the Piagetian cognitive stages may act as pacers for the development of the ego. More recent investigations have demonstrated the fact, not too surprising, that the logico-mathematical sub-line of cognitive development does not correlate significantly with ego development, while measures of socio-emotional intelligence do. E.g., J. Manners and K. Durkin. (2001). A critical review of the validity of ego development theory and its measurement. *Journal of Personality Assessment*, 77(3), pp. 541- 567.

15.   Page 35.

Chapter 6

1. C. T. Tart. (1975). *States of Consciousness*. New York: E.P. Dutton. Also retrieved on June 1, 2007, at http://www.druglibrary.org/special/tart/soc5.htm.

2. You now know from the fist two chapters that I mean states of *experience*, but let's not complicate things further by wrangling over language.

3. Steven LaBarge. (1988). "Lucid dreaming in western literature." In J. Gackenbach and S. LaBarge (Eds.). *Conscious Mind, Sleeping Brain*. (pp. 11- 26). New York: Plenum.

4. Consciousness researcher Charles Tart (1969) first identified these as "high dreams."

5. Allan Combs and Stanley Krippner (1998).

6. See, e.g., Combs & Krippner (1998); S. Krippner, F. Bogzaran, and A. P. De Carvalho. (2002); LaBarge (1988); and Tart (1969).

7. From his Gifford Lectures, given at the University of Edinburgh, and in 1902 to become his best-known book, *The Varieties of Religions Experience*; (1902/1929). New York: Modern Library, p. 278.

8. C. T. Tart. (1975). *States of Consciousness*. New York: E.P. Dutton.

9. E.g., Combs (2002) and Combs & Krippner (1999).

10. *Cybernetics* is a term dating from the mid-twentieth century that refers to the study of self-regulating systems. It is an important predecessor of the modern sciences of complexity, in which it is still included. Wikipedia defines cybernetics as "the study of communication and control, typically involving regulatory feedback in living organisms, machines and organizations, as well as their combinations." Retrieved on June 1, 2007, from http://en.wikipedia.org/wiki/Cybernetics.

11. E.g., see Michael Winkelman (2000).

12. Piaget's approach to the growth of knowledge through development is sometimes termed *developmental epistemology*.

13. Piaget's developmental stages are described in Chapters 4 and 5.

14. E.g., Barnes, (2000); Combs (2002), Combs & Krippner, (2003), Feuerstein, 1987; Wilber (1986, 1995).

15. Referring to San peoples of southern Africa.

16.   J. Campbell. (1988). *Historical Atlas of World Mythology, Vol. I: The Way of the Animal Powers; Part 1: Mythologies of the Primitive Hunters and Gathers*. New York: Harper & Row.

17.   Retrieved on June 1, 2007, from http://en.wikipedia.org/wiki/Tiamat and http://www.thenagain.info/Classes/Sources/BabylonianCreation.html.

18.   E.g., see Riane Eisler's classic book, *The Chalice and the Blade: Our History, Our Future*. San Francisco: Harper & Row.

Chapter 7

1.   J. M. Baldwin. (1930). *History of Psychology in Autobiography*. Worcester, MA: Clark University Press, p. 22. Also retrieved June 1, 2007, at http://psychclassics.yorku.ca/Baldwin/murchison.htm .

2.   Reproduced with the permission of Ken Wilber, from *Integral Psychology*; pp. 43–44.

3.   K. Wilber. (1999). *The Collected Works of Ken Wilber, Volume 4*. Boston: Shambhala, p. 459.

4.   W. G. Perry. (1999). *Forms of Ethical and Intellectual Development in the College Years*. San Francisco: Jossey-Bass Publishers. Though Perry's study focused on young men, broadly similar results have been found when women are studied as well, as described in the classic book by Mary Belenky, et al., (1987). *Women's Ways of Knowing*. New York: Basic Books.

5.   Thomas Kuhn. (1962). *The Structure of Scientific Revolutions*. Chicago: University of Chicago Press.

6.   R. Kegan. (1994). *In Over our Heads*. Cambridge: Harvard University Press.

7.   See, for example, the excellent little book by J. Sobel and P. Sobel. (1984). *The Hierarchy of Minds: The Mind Levels; A Compilation from the Works of Sri Aurobindo and The Mother*. Pondicherry, India: Sri Aurobindo Ashram Press.

8.   B. Ghiselin. (1955). *The Creative Process: A Symposium*. New York: New American Library, p. 36.

9.   Virtually all spiritual traditions emphasize the importance of selflessness

and compassion as a central aspect of attainment (Combs, 2002; Wilber, Engler, & Brown, 1986; Washburn, 1988; & Wilber, 2000), while modern research on the highest stages of ego development seems to point in the same direction (e.g., Cook-Greuter, 1999; Marko, 2006; & Pfaffenberger, 2007).

10.   K. Wilber. (1999). "Odyssey", *Collected works*. Vol. 2 , p. 41.

11.   Ken Wilber. (1980). *The Atman Project*. Wheaton, IL: Theosophical Publishing House, p. 68.

12.   Dante. (1900). *The Inferno, Purgatorio, and Paradiso: Text, with Translation by Carlyle*. London: Okey, and Wicksteed (Temple Classics). The 33rd canto of the *Paradiso*.

13.   *Auguries of Innocence* (1803).

14.   Sri Aurobindo. (1972). *The synthesis of yoga*. Pondicherry, India: All India Press, pp. 458–59.

15.   See *The Radiance of Being* for more details.

16.   K. Wilber. (1999). *One Taste*. Boston; Shambhala, pp. 148–151.

17.   Sri Aurobindo. (1974). *Guidance from Sri Aurobindo (Vol. 1)*. Pondicherry, India, p. 288.

18.   William Irwin Thompson. (1978). *Darkness and Scattered Light*. Garden City, NY: Anchor, p. 176.

19.   The principal vehicle for this transformation is the practice of Integral Yoga, followed by the work of Supramental Yoga.

20.   See, for instance, David Loy's *Nondual Reality: A Study in Comparative Philosophy*, or Peter Fenner's *Radiant Mind*.

21.   K. Wilber. (1999). Stages of Spirituality. *Collected Works*, vol. 4, pp. 361–362.

22.   From an interview published in *Quest*, 1994 Spring, pp. 43-46.

23.   Prominent developmental researchers such as L. Kohlberg (1981), Loevinger (1976), and Kegan (1994), for instance, have examined stages of growth beyond the ordinary, but have not pushed their investigations toward the upper limits of human possibilities.

24.   Susanne Cook-Greuter (1999).

25.   Loevinger (1976).

26.   Jenny Wade (1996).

27.   Susanne Cook-Greuter (1999), p. 49.

28.   Interestingly, this flow of experience is described in detail in the ancient Tibetan spiritual rDzogs-chen philosophy where is it associated with an entire process worldview. See, for example, Combs (2002), Guenther, H.V. (1989).

29.   R.D. Laing (1979), p. 82.

30.   Paul Marko (2006).

31.   Angela Pfaffenberger (2007).

32.   Seemingly contrary to these ideas, popular publications such as Arjuna Ardagh's *The Translucent Revolution* report many stories of sudden spiritual awakenings. However, these tend to be about people with long previous histories of spiritual searching or practice. Moreover, it is never clear without careful scrutiny whether such reports actually involve changes in developmental *structures*, changes of *states of consciousness* such as shifting to a subtle or causal ground of experience, or simply represent adjustments in attitude in which one, for example, releases burdensome ideas or beliefs as is often the case in psychotherapy.

33.   E.g., A. Combs, A. Pfaffenberger, and P. Marko (in preparation). *The Postconventional Personality: Empirical Perspectives on Higher Development.*

34.   Combs & Krippner (2003).

35.   E.g., Combs (2002) and Wilber (2006).

36.   E.g., Greeley & McCready (1975) and Piechowski (2000, 2001).

37.   Combs & Krippner (2003).

38.   I. Baruss. (2007). *Science as a Spiritual Practice*. Exeter, UK: Imprint Academic, p. 6.

39.   B. Roberts. (1993). *The Experience of No-Self: A Contemplative Journey.* Albany, New York: State University of New York.

40.   G. Krishna. (1997). *Kundalini: The Evolutionary Energy in Man.* Boston: Shambhala.

41.   I discuss a number of these in *The Radiance of Being*.

42.   A. Maslow. (1970). *Religion, Values and Peak Experiences.* New York: Viking.

43.   Nevertheless, it is certainly possible to make the case that a person having a peak experience has undergone a temporary shift in cognitive structure, perhaps precipitating a change in the pattern of the self as well. It is undeniable that during such experiences cognition undergoes significant alterations. In fact many of the latter were catalogued by Abraham Maslow in *Toward a Psychology of Being*.

44.   K. Wilber. (2006). *Integral Spirituality*. Boston: Shambhala.

45.   E.g., K. Wilber. (2000b). *Integral Psychology*. Boston: Shambhala.

46.   With the permission of Ken Wilber, from *Integral Spirituality*.

47.   J. Fowler. *Stages of Faith*, San Francisco: Harper and Row, 1971.

Chapter 8

1.   I have described this history in more detail in *The Radiance of Being*.

2.   H. Bergson. (1907/1983). *Creative Evolution*. (A. Mitchell, Trans.). Lanham, MD: University Press of America Bergson, p. 179.

3.   P. Teilhard de Chardin. (1959/1961). *The Phenomenon of Man*. New York: Harper & Row. (Originally written between 1938 and 1940 but suppressed by the Catholic Church until the French edition was released in 1955.)

4.   Aurobindo. (1972). *The Synthesis of Yoga*. Pondicherry, India: All India Press, p. 47

5.   These levels correspond surprisingly well with the vehicles and subtle realms of Vedanta.

6.   A. Combs. (2001). Inner and outer realities: Jean Gebser in a cultural/ historical perspective. *The Journal of Conscious Evolution*. http://www. cejournal.org/GRD/Realities.htm.

7.   Social Darwinism is a label often used to characterize a variety of nineteenth and early twentieth century writers who argued in favor of the superiority of certain races and cultures—mostly white and European—on the basis of their greater perceived success. The notion of "success," often taken for granted by such writers, was based on an optimistic appraisal of the recent European Industrial Revolution.

8.   J. Jaynes. (1976). *The Origin of Consciousness in the Breakdown of the Bicameral Mind*. Boston: Houghton Mifflin.

9.   M. Berman. (1989). *Coming to Our Senses: Body and Spirit in the Hidden History of the West.* New York: Simon & Schuster

10.   E.g., see Berman (1989) and Anderson (1990).

11.   Said to have been the father of humanism.

12.   Imagining for the moment that the events depicted in the *Odyssey* are historically accurate.

13.   Unless you are a rabbit.

14.   K. Wilber. (2006). *Integral spirituality.* Boston: Shambhala.

15.   Wilber first introduced the eight perspective model in detail in *Integral Spirituality.*

16.   Reproduced with permission from Ken Wilber.

17.   Indeed, the great contradiction in the traditional idea of the detached observer scientist is the notion that he or she can stand outside of any perspective at all and simply view the phenomena under investigation with pure detachment.

18.   In fact, the idea of "public observation" was an important aspect of the early behaviorist school of psychology.

19.   As a point of interest, much brain science today utilizes a variety of methods for imaging electrical activity in the living brain. This approach actually represents a Zone 6, or at best Zone 8, approach. This is because its goal is to disclose areas of the brain that are active in one or another type of activity, almost as if dissecting them out, and illustrating them to an outside view. While research is making significant contributions to our understanding of the brain, its results are usually unable to disclose the actual processes that underlie, e.g., one or another kinds of mental process.

20.   See Chapter 7.

21.   One wonders if the attacks on phenomenology and subjectivity in philosophy delivered by Michel Foucault during the 1960s, and widely accepted by European intellectuals, discouraged serious exploration of the inner aspects of collective experience as well as undercutting the legitimacy of subjectivity in general. The essential argument was that conscious experience is so influenced by cultural, linguistic, and historical factors that the examination of experience itself has no

authority. See especially his 1966 *Les Mots et les choses. Une archéologie des sciences humaines*, published in English in 1970 as *The Order of Things: An Archaeology of the Human Sciences*.

22. A fascinating take on the modern notion of collective consciousness involves a situation known in the field of artificial intelligence as *Estimation of Distribution Algorithms* (EDA) in which a group of individual minds can mutually access each other's knowledge (schemas or in AI terms "algorithms"). The result is a kind of collective mind in which the best approaches to a problem can be quickly compared and the best ones selected. In the meantime, the individual minds within this community do not lose their own integrity, but benefit from access to the larger field of knowledge held within the group. (See Goertzel, 2006). The implications of this idea for human psychology range from a deeper understanding of archetypes to how collective wisdom is held in primary cultures such as the Australian Aborigines. For more reflections on this topic see my paper with Stanley Krippner (2008).

23. Christopher C. Cowan and Natasha Todorovic, eds. (2005) *The Never Ending Quest: Dr. Clare W. Graves Explores Human Nature.* Santa Barbara, CA: ECLET Publishing.

24. *Guernica,* finished in 1937, is considered by many to be the greatest antiwar artwork of all time. The painting represents the recent bombing of the Spanish town of Guernica by the Nazi air force. It was the first time in modern history that a town of civilians was brutally and utterly destroyed in war, and for most of the world it was completely unexpected.

Chapter 9

1. *Kenshō* is similar to a *satori* (enlightenment) experience, but is not permanent as is the former.

2. To be more accurate, such complex systems tend to form *holarchies*, which incorporate hierarchical chains of causation or command.

3. Interestingly, a similar historical sequence was proposed by the eighteenth century Italian philosopher Giambattista Vico, and by ancient historians such as the Roman poet Ovid who claimed that he based his model on an even earlier Egyptian history. These are discussed in more detail in *The Radiance of Being*.

4.   Note that this does not mean their actions as shamans were ineffectual. On the contrary, Gebser believed those who live in a magical world—that is, live through the magical structure of consciousness—regularly experience genuine magical phenomena such as telepathy and synchronicities.

5.   E.g., S. Krippner. (2002). "Conflicting perspectives on shamans and shamanism: Points and counterpoints." *American Psychologist, 57*, 962–977.

6.   See Tables 7.1 and 7.2 in chapter 7.

7.   K. Wilber. (2000a). *A Theory of Everything: An Integral Vision for Business, Politics, Science, and Spirituality.* Boston: Shambhala.

8.   A period when fascinating, brilliant, and sometimes eccentric figures ranging from William James to Madame Blavatsky peopled the American spiritual landscape.

9.   The fact that the word "enlightenment" does not exist, even in direct translation, in traditional Eastern texts was first pointed out to me by the great Asian scholar Herbert Guenther. For this reason he never used the word "enlightenment" in any of his translations of Eastern spiritual texts.

10.   K. Wilber. (2006). *Integral Spirituality.* Boston: Shambhala, p. 248.

11.   The numbers of such scholars are too great to mention individually and, consistent with their relativism, none are remarkably outstanding.

12.   Here I have not emphasized the considerable significance of ethnic or linguistic aspects of conscious experience because my interest in this book has been to search for what is universal in human experience. However, I recognize that in day-to-day living, and even in the realm of religious and mystical experience, these are important ingredients. As we noted in the discussion of the Wilber-Combs matrix, they are especially important for how a person reports and frames a religious or mystical experience. All this, of course, has to do with a person's developmental stage as well as his or her cultural context. I note this because the latter is almost always omitted from relativistic explanations of religious experience.

13.   D. Zindell. (1998). *War in Heaven; Book Three of a Requiem for Homo Sapiens.* London: HarperCollins, p. 790.

Bibliography

Anderson, W.T. (1990). *Reality Isn't What It Used to Be: Theatrical Politics, Ready-to-Wear Religion, Global Myths, Primitive Chic, and Other Wonders of the Postmodern World.* New York: Harper & Row.

Ardagh, A. (2005). *The Translucent Revolution: How People Just Like You are Waking Up and Changing the World.* Novato, CA: New World Library.

Atkins, P. (2004). *Galileo's Finger: The Ten Great Ideas of Science.* NYC: Oxford University Press.

Aurobindo. (1972). *The Synthesis of Yoga.* Pondicherry, India: All India Press.

Aurobindo. (1974). *Guidance from Sri Aurobindo (Vol. 1).* Pondicherry, India: All India Press.

Baldwin, J.M. (1930). *History of Psychology in Autobiography.* Worcester, MA: Clark University Press. Retrieved on June 1, 2007 from http://psychclassics.yorku.ca/Baldwin/murchison.htm.

Barnes, H.B. (2000). *Stages of Thought: The Co-evolution of Religious Thought and Science.* New York: Oxford University Press.

Bergson, H. (1907/1983). *Creative Evolution.* (A. Mitchell, Trans.). Lanham, MD: University Press of America.

Berman, M. (1989). *Coming to Our Senses: Body and Spirit in the Hidden History of the West.* New York: Simon & Schuster.

Baruss, I. (2007). *Science as a Spiritual Practice.* Exeter, UK: Imprint Academic.

Bly, R. (1988). *A Little Book on the Human Shadow.* San Francisco: Harper & Row.

Broughton, J. (1987). *Critical Theories of Psychological Development.* New York: Springer.

Campbell, J. (1988). *Historical Atlas of World Mythology, Vol. I: The Way of the Animal Powers; Part 1: Mythologies of the Primitive Hunters and Gatherers.* New York: Harper & Row.

Carroll, L. (1865/2004). *Alice in Wonderland.* New York: Random House, Gramercy.

Goertzel, B. (2006). *The Hidden Pattern: A Patternist Philosophy of Mind.* Boca Raton, FL: BrownWalker.

Combs, A. (2001). Inner and outer realities: Jean Gebser in a cultural/ historical perspective. *The Journal of Conscious Evolution.* http:// www.cejournal.org/GRD/Realities.htm.

Combs, A. (2002). *The Radiance of Being: Understanding the Grand Integral Vision; Living the Integral Life.* St Paul, MN: Paragon House.

Combs, A. and Krippner, S. (1998). Dream sleep and waking reality: A dynamical view of two states of consciousness. In S. Hameroff, A.W. Kaszniak, and A.C. Scott (Eds.). *Toward a Science of Consciousness: The Second Tucson Discussions and Debates.* (pp. 487–93). Cambridge, MA: MIT Press.

Combs, A., and Krippner, S. (1999). "Spiritual growth and the evolution of consciousness: Complexity, evolution, and the farther reaches of human nature." *The International Journal of Transpersonal Studies, 18*(1), pp. 9-19.

Combs, A., and Krippner, S. (2003). "Process, structure, and form: An evolutionary transpersonal psychology of consciousness." *International Journal of Transpersonal Studies. 22,* 47-60. [Also available at http://www.sourceintegralis.org/Process,%20 Structure,%20and%20Form.pdf].

Combs, A. and Krippner, S. (2008). "Collective consciousness and the social brain." *Journal of Consciousness Studies, 15,* pp. 264-276.

Cook-Greuter, S. (1999). *Postautonomous Ego Development: A Study of its Nature and Measurement.* Harvard University: A doctoral dissertation. Available from the author: cookgsu@aol.com .

Eisler, R. (1987). *The Chalice and the Blade: Our History, Our Future.* San Francisco: Harper & Row.

Fenner, P. (2007). *Radiant Mind.* Louisville, CO: Sounds True.

Feuerstein, G. (Trans. 1979/1989). *The Yoga-Sutra of Patanjali: A New Translation and Commentary.* Rochester, Vermont: Inner Traditions.

Feuerstein, G. (1987). *Structures of Consciousness: The Genius of Jean Gebser.* Lower Lake, CA: Integral Publishing.

Foucault, M. (1970). *The order of things: An Archaeology of the Human Sciences.* New York: Pantheon.

Fowler, J. (1970). *Stages of Faith.* San Francisco: Harper & Row.

Greeley, A., and W. McCready. (1975). Are we a nation of mystics? In D. Goleman and R. J. Davidson (Eds.), *Consciousness, Brain, States of Awareness, and Mysticism.* (pp. 175-183). New York: Harper & Row.

Guenther, H.V. (1989). *From Reductionism to Creativity: rDzogs-chen and the New Sciences of Mind.* Boston: Shambhala.

Gupta, B. (2003). *Cit Consciousness.* New York: Oxford University Press.

Hughes, R. (1928). *A High Wind in Jamaica: The Innocent Voyage.* New York: New American Library.

James, W. (1890/1981). *The Principles of Psychology.* Cambridge, MA: Harvard University Press.

James, W. (1902/1929). *The Varieties of Religious Experience.* New York: Modern Library.

James, W. (1911/1996). *Some Problems of Philosophy; A Beginning of an Introduction to Philosophy.* Lincoln, NE: University of Nebraska Press.

James, W. (1912/1996). *Essays in Radical Empiricism.* Lincoln, NE: University of Nebraska Press.

Jaynes, J. (1976). *The Origin of Consciousness in the Breakdown of the Bicameral Mind.* Boston: Houghton Mifflin.

Kegan, R.(1995). *In Over Our Heads: The Mental Demands of Modern Life*. Cambridge, MA: Harvard University Press.

Kohlberg, L. (1981). *Essays on Moral Development (Vol.1)*. San Francisco: Harper.

Krippner, S., F. Bogzaran, and A. P. De Carvalho. (2002). *Extraordinary Dreams and How to Work with Them*. Albany, New York: State University of New York.

Krishna, G. (1997). *Kundalini: The Evolutionary Energy in Man*. Boston: Shambhala.

Kuhn, T. (1962). *The Structure of Scientific Revolutions*. Chicago: University of Chicago Press.

LaBarge, S. (1988). Lucid dreaming in western literature. In J. Gackenbach and S. LaBarge (Eds.), *Conscious Mind, Sleeping Brain*. (pp.11- 26). New York: Plenum.

Laing, R. D. (1979). *Knots*. New York: Pantheon Books.

Locke, J. (1689/2007). *An Essay Concerning Human Understanding*. Pomona, CA: Pomona Press.

Loevinger, J. (1976). *Ego Development*. San Francisco: Jossey-Bass.

Loy, D. (1997). *Nondual Reality: A Study in Comparative Philosophy*. Amherst, NY: Humanity.

Manners, J., and K. Durkin. (2001). A critical review of the validity of ego development theory and its measurement. *Journal of Personality Assessment, 77*(3), 541- 567

Mahler, M. S. (1979). *Separation-Individuation: The Selected Papers of Margret S. Mahler Vol. II*. New York: Jason Aronson.

Mahler, M. S., F. Pine, and A. Bergman. (1975). *The Psychological Birth of the Human Infant*. New York: Basic Books.

Marko, P. W. (2006). *Exploring Facilitative Agents That Allow Ego Development to Occur*. Saybrook Graduate School: A doctoral dissertation. Available from the author at http://mindfulendeavors. com/books.htm.

Maslow, A. (1962). *Toward a Psychology of Being*. Princeton, NJ: Van Nostrand.

Metzner, R. (1998). *The Unfolding Self: Varieties of Transformative Experience*. San Rafael, CA: Origin.

Pfaffenberger, A. (2007). *Exploring the Path to Self-Actualization: A Qualitative Study*. Saybrook Graduate School: A doctoral dissertation available from the author at Pwmarko@aol.com.

Piechowski, M. M. (2000). Childhood experiences and spiritual giftedness. *Advanced Development*, 9, 65–90.

Piechowski, M. M. (2001). Childhood spirituality. *Journal of Transpersonal Psychology*, 33, 1–15.

Pret, R. (2005). *Onflow: Dynamics of Consciousness and Experience*. Cambridge, MA: MIT Press.

Roberts, B. (1992). *The Path to No-Self: Life at the Center*. Albany, New York: State University of New York.

Roberts, B. (1993). *The Experience of No-Self: A Contemplative Journey*. Albany, New York: State University of New York.

Silburn, L. (1988). *Kundalini: The Energy of the Depths*. (J. Gontier, Trans.). Albany, NY: State University of New York Press.

Singer, D. G., and Revenson, T. A. (1998). *A Piaget Primer: How a Child Thinks*. Madison, CT: International Universities Press.

Spencer-Brown, G. (1979). *Laws of Form*. New York: E. P. Dutton.

Stanley, M. (1993). *Emanuel Swedenborg*. Berkeley, CA: North Atlantic Books.

Tart, C. T. (1969). The high dream. In C. Tart (Ed.). *Altered States of Consciousness*. (pp. 171- 176). New York: Doubleday.

Tart, C. T. (1975). *States of Consciousness*. NY: E.P. Dutton.

Teilhard de Chardin, P. (1959/1961). *The Phenomenon of Man*. New York: Harper & Row.

Thompson, W. I. (1978). *Darkness and Scattered Light*. Garden City, New York: Anchor.

Underhill, E. (1911/1961). *Mysticism*. New York: E.P. Dutton.

von Boris Hennig, A. (1974). *Was bedeutet 'conscientia' bei Descartes?* Der Fakultät für Sozialwissenschalften und Philosopie der Universität Leipzig. Dissertation. Retrieved June 1, 2007, from http://www.borishennig.de/texte/descartes/diss/.

Wade, J. (1996). *Changes of Mind: A Holonomic Theory of the Evolution of Consciousness*. Albany, NY: State University of New York Press.

Washburn, M. (1988). *The Ego and the Dynamic Ground*. Albany, NY: State University of New York Press.

Wells, C. (Ed.). (1902). *A Nonsense Anthology*. New York: Scribner's.

Whitehead, A.N.. (1929/1978). *Process and Reality: An Essay in Cosmology*. New York: Collier Macmillan.

Wilber, K. (1996, May). The kosmos according to Ken Wilber: An interview with Robin Kornman. *Shambhala Sun*. Retrieved June 1, 2007, from http://www.shambhalasun.com/Archives/Features/1996/Sept96/KenWilber.htm.

Wilber, K. (1980). *The Atman Project*. Wheaton, IL: Theosophical Publishing House.

Wilber, K. (1983). *Eye to Eye*. New York: Doubleday/Anchor.

Wilber, K. (1986). The spectrum of development. In K. Wilber, J. Engler, and D. P. Brown (Eds.), *Transformations of Consciousness* (pp. 65-106). Boston: Shambhala.

Wilber, K. (1995). *Sex, Ecology, Spirituality: The Spirit of Evolution*. Boston: Shambhala.

Wilber, K. (1999). *One Taste*. Boston: Shambhala.

Wilber, K. (2000a). *A Theory of Everything: An Integral Vision for Business, Politics, Science, and Spirituality*. Boston: Shambhala.

Wilber, K. (2000b). *Integral Psychology*. Boston: Shambhala.

Wilber, K. (2006). *Integral Spirituality*. Boston: Shambhala.

Wilber, K., J. Engler, and D. P. Brown. (Eds.). (1986). *Transformations of Consciousness*. Boston: Shambhala.

Winkelman, M. (2000). *Shamanism: The Neural Ecology of Consciousness and Healing*. Westport CT: Bergin & Garvey.

Winograd, T. (1972). *Understanding Natural Language*. New York: Academic Press.

Zindell, D. (1998). *War in Heaven; Book Three of a Requiem for Homo Sapiens*. London: HarperCollins.

Index